What People Think Principals Do

Sharon H. Pristash

A SCARECROWEDUCATION BOOK

The Scarecrow Press, Inc.
Lanham, Maryland, and Oxford
2002

A SCARECROWEDUCATION BOOK

Published in the United States of America
by Scarecrow Press, Inc.
A Member of the Rowman & Littlefield Publishing Group
4720 Boston Way, Lanham, Maryland 20706
www.scarecroweducation.com

PO Box 317
Oxford
OX2 9RU, UK

Copyright © 2002 by Sharon H. Pristash

All rights reserved. No part of this publication may be reproduced, stored in a retrieval system, or transmitted in any form or by any means, electronic, mechanical, photocopying, recording, or otherwise, without the prior permission of the publisher.

British Library Cataloguing in Publication Information Available

Library of Congress Cataloging-in-Publication Data

Pristash, Sharon H., 1963–
  What people think principals do / Sharon H. Pristash.
    p. cm.
  "A ScarecrowEducation book."
  ISBN 0-8108-4468-0 (cloth : alk. paper)—ISBN 0-8108-4469-9 (pbk. : alk. paper)
  1. School principals—United States. 2. Educational leadership—United States. I. Title.
  LB2831.92 .P77 2002
  371.2'012—dc21   2002005355

∞™ The paper used in this publication meets the minimum requirements of American National Standard for Information Sciences—Permanence of Paper for Printed Library Materials, ANSI/NISO Z39.48-1992.
Manufactured in the United States of America.

To my parents,
who gave me a happy childhood

Contents

Acknowledgments		vii
1	Introduction	1
2	What Students Think Principals Do	7
3	What Parents Think Principals Do	28
4	What Teachers Think Principals Do	45
5	What Other Community Members Think Principals Do	61
6	How Hollywood Portrays Principals	73
7	Principals' Reactions to What People Think Principals Do	93
8	Final Thoughts	102
About the Author		107

Acknowledgments

I want to thank all the students, parents, teachers, and community members who willingly gave of their time and enthusiastically shared their thoughts with me. This book is as much theirs as it is mine. I extend a special thanks to my principal colleagues who helped this book to answer so much more than my initial questions. Several friends and colleagues reviewed the drafts of this manuscript in its early stages and provided helpful and honest feedback. I am indebted to those people for keeping me on track and encouraging me when the going got rough. Thanks to Chuck Frederick, Cindy Graham, Emma Chavez, and Monte Wittman.

I wish to acknowledge the assistance of Dr. Tom Koerner, editorial director at Scarecrow Press. His enthusiasm, insight and patience encouraged me throughout this journey. Appreciation is also due my former graduate school professor and now friend, Dr. Robert Brown at the University of St. Thomas in St. Paul, Minnesota. It was at his suggestion that I considered writing a book about a topic he knew was close to my heart.

Finally, I wish to express gratitude to my husband, Robert, and all my family and friends who encouraged me throughout this project and never doubted that I would finish it.

Chapter One

Introduction

WHY THIS BOOK?

When I proposed the idea for this book, I had recently completed my third year as an elementary school principal. At that time many things had surprised me about the job, but none so much as the perceptions people seemed to have about it. Several types of experiences tended to provoke contemplation. Many times I would be in my office—hands on the keyboard, phone in my ear, or paperwork piled around me—and someone would come to the door and ask, "Are you busy?" I often bit my tongue so as not to reply, "Of course I'm busy. I'm always busy." At those times I wondered what people think I do all day. Is it possible some might think there are actually times when I'm not busy, when all my work is done?

Another curious experience is the phone call from someone inquiring about the week's lunch menu or the due date for his or her child's science project. In these cases I think to myself, "Do people expect me to keep track of all these details?" Then there are the teacher requests like, "Why don't we change our schedule so we start a half hour earlier and get done a half hour earlier?" I only wish it was within my power to control the transportation schedule. Finally, there is the child who—in all seriousness—tells me something like, "We get to have a non-uniform day on the last day of school." I smile and say, "I know, honey," while to myself I add, "Gee, I wonder whose idea that was?"

While sharing these experiences with a principal colleague of mine I found that I am not alone. She stated, "I am occasionally surprised about comments that suggest to me how little is understood about the principal's role." She shared an example regarding a teacher she is encouraging to pursue principal licensure. The teacher told my colleague she isn't interested in becoming a principal because she doesn't like working with data and money. It surprised this principal that an experienced teacher actually thinks that working with data and money are key elements of the principal job.

Like me, my colleague has also experienced instances where people think the principal's responsibilities extend to every possible facet of school life. She, too, has had to tell parents that transportation issues are not within her jurisdiction. She humorously related a call from a parent inquiring if she knew the source of the worksheet the parent's child had brought home. My colleague's incredulous response to me was, "I have about 500 students who are each given multiple homework assignments. Does this parent really believe I know how a teacher selected this single sheet on this particular homework assignment?"

These types of experiences suggested to me that the job of the principal is perceived by others in many different ways. Some people seem to think the principal knows everything that is happening in the school at any given moment and should have a ready answer to every question. Others appear to think that whatever principals do all day is completely unconnected to the rest of the school. We are perceived as all-powerful and completely out of touch—at the same time. It seems to be the nature of the job. Principals are revered by some and feared by others. Some want to turn to the principal to solve every little issue, while others would just as soon avoid the principal as much as possible.

Rather than simply ponder this phenomenon, I decided to examine the many perceptions people have of principals. I could continue wondering what people think I do, or I could simply find out. From my doctoral research I have learned there is a fair amount of literature devoted to "what principals do." From what I can determine, there is none devoted to "what people *think* principals do." That is how the seeds of curiosity grew into the idea for a book, which I hope will appeal to anyone with an interest in the principalship.

SOME BACKGROUND

Much of the literature on the role of principals stresses the scope, complexity, and ambiguity of the job. Many new and veteran principals remark that one cannot truly know what it means to be a principal until you are one. At the same time, most people have developed their own perceptions of what a principal is and does. Their notions of the principalship may include ideas about the tasks principals perform, the skills principals should have, and the types of people who are drawn to the principalship. The groups of people whose perceptions most interested me as I outlined this book were students, teachers, parents, non-parent community members, and the media.

One thing all the groups above have in common is their experiences as students—in most cases, twelve years of schooling in elementary and secondary schools. Because most people in our country have had direct experience with a principal or principals, they have developed a worldview of the role of the principal. This worldview may or may not correspond to the realities of the principalship as perceived through the eyes of principals themselves.

This book describes the various perceptions of the principalship from the viewpoint of people both close to and distant from the role. Through interviews with students, teachers, parents, and community members, I compiled many pages of responses to the following questions:

- What is a principal?
- What does a principal do?
- Does a school need a principal? Why or why not?
- *Who* needs the principal?
- Why do you think people choose to become principals?
- What do you think would be hardest about the job?
- What do you think is the most important thing that principals do?
- Without a principal, what do you think it would be like at school?
- Would you want to be a principal?
- Can you think of another job in the world that you would compare to a principal? Being a principal is like being . . .
- Think about the principals you know—is there anything you think they don't do that maybe they should?
- Who was your favorite principal? What made him/her your favorite?
- What do you think people learn about in "principal school?" What knowledge and skills are developed through principal training programs?

The responses I received to these questions are discussed in the following chapters. In addition to summarizing what students, teachers, parents, and community members perceive about the principal role, I offer some implications these perceptions might have for members of this profession—or those who aspire to it.

I also viewed many movies to discover how principals are portrayed in film. I chose to include Hollywood's perceptions of principals because the entertainment media is a powerful force in our society today. The question often debated is, does the entertainment media *reflect* society's values and perceptions or does it *shape* them? I narrowed my focus to the media of film, though the same investigation could be made of the perceptions portrayed through television shows and fictional literature—especially those aimed at children and young adults.

Finally, this book includes the viewpoints of practicing or former principals. A major goal of the book is to compare and contrast various perceptions of principals' work. A second goal is to describe the extent to which these perceptions correspond to the "real world" of the principalship. I dedicate one chapter to principals' reflections on their practices and their reactions to the perceptions described in the other chapters.

WHO MIGHT READ THIS BOOK?

This book is targeted at practicing principals—both novice and veteran. I hope it will help principals to better understand how others might view them and their role within the school. This in turn will assist principals in relating to the many stakeholders for whom they work. Perhaps principals will examine their practices to determine how their actions and words may be perceived by others and possibly influence people's perceptions of the principal's role in general. Working principals will be in a position to improve their relationships and effectiveness, if they more clearly communicate their roles to others. And this book will extend most people's understanding of those roles. If nothing else, I think principals will find some entertainment value in reading people's views about their job.

Aspiring principals will also be interested in this book for the reasons described above. Current training programs for school administrators include an emphasis on community building and shared decision making.

These processes are more effective when the leadership and the stakeholders have a common frame of reference. In other words, principals and soon-to-be principals might be more effective leaders if there is some alignment between what *they* think I do and what *I* think I do. This book also provides aspiring principals a peek at what the principalship entails—the many expectations people have of you and the many hats you may be asked to wear in the day-to-day operation of a school.

Finally, this book will appeal to anyone with an interest in education or with a connection to schools. Each school in the United States is under the direct leadership of a principal. If we hope to improve schools, we must work with the onsite school leaders, the principals. The better we understand the role of leadership in our schools, the better we can build the necessary relationships and vision needed to help schools meet the needs of students and of society. Reading this book will increase peoples' ability to evaluate the effectiveness of a school principal or the qualifications of those seeking a principal position. This book provides insight into ways colleges and universities can improve principal training programs. Any person who reads this book will develop a better understanding of what principals do and the impact (for good or bad) a principal has on a school community.

KEEPING IT IN PERSPECTIVE

There are some important facts the reader should know about this book. The perceptions discussed in this book are based on interviews and conversations with over seventy people. Because I live in the Midwest, the people I interviewed are also Midwesterners, though they live in different communities—including cities, small towns, and rural areas. I'm quite certain there are many more perceptions to be uncovered by those with connections to schools in large urban areas on either coast or schools in the south and southwest.

Second, although the majority of the people interviewed are not directly connected to my particular school, all of my sources know that I am a principal. Regardless of my attempts to encourage candid replies to my questions, there remains the possibility that some respondents might have considered my reaction as they shared their ideas and attitudes. As the interviewer, however, I am confident that most of the information I uncovered reflects my sources' true perceptions of the principalship. The variety of questions I asked targeted people's perceptions from different angles, and thus I was not limited by answers to the simple question, What do principals do? For example, asking what it would be like at school without a principal tended to elicit a gut-level response and unearthed some revealing notions about what principals do.

Finally, this book has a specific focus—perceptions of the principalship. That is not to suggest that the principal's job alone is prey to particular assumptions or misconceptions. I do not discount the fact that other professions or positions are also open to many interpretations. What people think principals do is of no more significance than what people think *anyone* else does. But it *is* of particular significance to those with a personal interest in the role of the principal, and it is those people for whom this book is written.

Chapter Two

What Students Think Principals Do

INTRODUCTION

Of the many people I interviewed for this book, the students were by far the most fun. I found their candid reflections on the principalship to be both entertaining and insightful. In some ways the students I spoke with viewed the principal job much as I thought they would, but in many instances I was surprised by the depth of their perceptions. I was also surprised by the level of appreciation some students have for the principal role.

For this chapter I interviewed students from five to nineteen years old. They attend different schools in different communities. I asked each student a series of questions I hoped would uncover their attitudes and beliefs about the principal role. I do not include responses to all the questions in this chapter, and limit my discussion to those I felt were most illustrative of students' perceptions of the principal role.

The students' responses suggest a great deal about their individual student experiences in school—and a great deal about the types of principals they have known. In this chapter I will share these revealing perceptions, often in their own words, concluding with a brief discussion of what I learned from these students and the implications of what that information might have for other principals and those who aspire to that role.

WHAT IS A PRINCIPAL?

After the customary small talk to break the ice, every interview began with this simple question, and it elicited some very simple answers. I was not surprised to find that most students consider the principal to be the person who:

- is the boss of the school
- is in charge of the school
- runs the school
- is the head of the school
- makes up the rules
- tells kids what to do
- makes sure everyone gets along
- you go to if you're in trouble

Some more descriptive terms were the *head honcho, numero uno,* and *highest authority.* Student definitions focused almost exclusively on the concepts of boss and disciplinarian. The principal runs the school and keeps order. Only one student—a fourth-grade girl—deviated from this theme and defined the principal as *someone who takes care of the school.*

> The most unique response to the question, "What is a principal?": "The top banana." (third grade student)

WHAT DO PRINCIPALS DO?

This question was intended to generate a host of responses, and with most students it did. Some were initially concerned with giving the "right" answers, looking to me for confirmation when they hazarded a guess. I soon learned to follow this question with, "What kinds of things have you *seen* principals do at school? What kinds of things do you *think* they are doing during the day when you don't see them?" As one might expect, the age of the student had some bearing on the number and types of responsibilities they perceived in the principal role.

Students from kindergarten to about second grade supplied very concrete accounts of what principals do. They observed that principals walk around the halls, do announcements, sit at a desk filling out papers, talk to kids who are bad, talk to teachers, and sometimes come into the classroom. One second-grade student matter-of-factly stated that "sometimes he has to take a bathroom break." For the most part, younger students could describe what they *saw* principals do, but had few notions about what the principal did otherwise. A typical response was, "They do work," but what that work might entail was lost to most students this age.

Students in the middle and upper elementary grades repeated all of the observations above ("walk around the halls" was the most popular response) but focused more heavily on the disciplinary tasks: *keep order, boss kids around, set rules, handle naughty kids, boss people around,* and *make sure kids don't skip.* Yet they also inferred that the principal job encompasses other tasks: *telling teachers what to do, talking to parents, taking care of problems, making decisions, doing paperwork, working on the computer,* and *giving advice.*

In one sense, junior high students tend to have a unique view of the principal role. Like elementary students they had a lot to say about the disciplinary aspects of the job, but tended to add an adolescent twist. Some typical responses include: *they do annoying things, write up rules just to bug us,* and *walk around the school looking for trouble* or *getting students in trouble.* To anyone who has experience with early adolescent students, it might be no surprise that they perceive "getting in trouble" not as something students *do* so much as something done *to* them. The responses above (mainly from seventh and eighth grade students) also illustrate another developmental characteristic—the desire to shock or "get a rise." I discerned that some of these students gave tongue-in-cheek responses just to see my reaction. Would this have been the case if my principal status were not known to these students? Or was it merely my *adult* status that provoked eyebrow-raising responses? Possibly a little of both.

Their responses weren't limited to this variety, however. By seventh and eighth grade, students also recognize that a principal is responsible for many things. While younger students could only say that principals do paperwork or office work, these older students could describe what that work entails: *printing up notes and forms, writing reports, organizing school events, emailing other schools, signing things, writing checks,* and *keeping the school up-to-date.* A few students in this age group even identified some of the 'bigger picture" things that principals do: *make decisions, take care of problems, counsel students and parents, motivate and encourage students, meet with teachers to discuss what they are teaching, raise funds,* and *advertise the school.* I was surprised by the level of awareness and even appreciation exhibited by students in this group. Although they tend to focus first on the disciplinary role, they recognize that a principal does many things—and some of them are even good for kids!

High school students' ideas of what principals do tended to run to extremes. Some had very little to say about what principals do, while others rattled off extensive lists. Not surprisingly, those who gave limited responses not only didn't know what principals *do*, they didn't know their principal. A ninth-grade student told me, "I've only seen my principal once this year—in her office. I don't know her name. Similarly, one tenth-grade student admitted, "I don't even know what my principal looks like." A recent high school graduate was frustrated throughout the interview and told me more than once, "I just honestly don't know their job."

One might wonder, are these students the victims of oversized high schools, where the principal is too overworked to come out of the office? Or do these principals simply opt for low visibility by their own choice? Might it be the *students'* lack of participation in school that causes them to have such little contact with their principal? Each of these students attends high school in a different city, so their responses are not illustrative of only one school. Whatever the reason for this phenomenon, it was only at the high school level that I found students who pointedly told me they didn't know their principal.

At the other end of the spectrum are the high school students who have many ideas about the principal job. They were able to identify all the tasks mentioned by the younger students and recognized several more. Once again, disciplining students, planning assemblies and walking around the school appear to be a major part of the job from a student perspective. But these older students also perceived that principals: *organize and go to meetings, do budgets, resolve conflicts, try to relate to students, interview people for jobs, evaluate their employees, converse with students,* and *get calls from concerned parents.* I began to think some of these students had been peeking in my office and taking notes. I was surprised at their ability to understand the multifaceted nature of the principal role.

Although these first two questions helped me to understand the student view of the principalship, I felt it was only the tip of the iceberg—the obvious stuff sitting on the surface. I was certain that students possessed more deeply embedded assumptions or beliefs about principals and their work, and the remaining interview questions were intended to unearth those assumptions and beliefs.

> The most unique response to the question "What do principals do?": "They go home and make lists of stuff they can do to kids to be mean." (eighth-grade student, surprise, surprise!)

WHY DOES A SCHOOL NEED A PRINCIPAL?

Before asking why does a school need a principal, I asked the more direct question, "*Does* a school need a principal?" All the students I interviewed, regardless of age, answered "yes" with very little hesitation. The next question was, "Why?" The replies to this question helped me to understand another piece of the student perspective. The reasons a school needs a principal reveal additional beliefs that students have about the role.

Most students identified student discipline as the main reason schools need principals. In their own words, a school needs a principal: *to keep order, to discipline kids who get in trouble, to set the rules, to keep kids from going out and getting in trouble, to suspend really bad kids*. Some students explained why a school needs a principal by suggesting what it would be like without one: *or else there would be no rules; everybody would be pinching or kicking or hitting everybody; otherwise everyone would be out of control; if not, the kids would be all rammy and break windows and be all hyper*. Later in the interview I specifically asked students to speculate about a school without a principal. I didn't expect students to offer these ideas without solicitation.

Other reasons a school needs a principal are related to organization and management: *to make sure everything runs smoothly, to keep the school organized, to keep everything in order, to make sure everything's okay*. A seventh-grade student explained, "A school needs a principal to organize the whole school. It would be too much for the teachers." Another seventh grade reply was, "He/She is the one that brings everything together." I was surprised to find that students place so much responsibility for the school's successful operation on the principal. I truly expected that at least some students, especially older ones, would think that the principal was fairly expendable. Yet even the three students who rarely saw their principal or didn't know their principal's name agreed that the school needs him/her. One high school student elaborated on her affirmative reply, stating, "It is possible for a school to run without a principal, but it's not logical."

A pattern I saw in these responses is that very few students referred directly to the educational mission of the school. One sixth-grade student mentioned that a school needs a principal "to make sure teachers are doing their jobs." Similarly, a seventh-grade student observed that "the principal tells the teachers what to do." These were the only two responses that touched on the principal's role in the teaching and learning processes. This suggested to me that students see the principal as primarily a disciplinarian and a manager, not as an educational leader.

> The most unique response to the question "Why does a school need a principal?": "They must need them; otherwise they wouldn't have one." (twelfth-grade student)

WHO NEEDS THE PRINCIPAL?

It might seem redundant to follow the previous question with the question of who needs the principal, but I didn't want to *assume* that students don't connect the principal role to teaching and learning. By asking students to identify specific groups of people within or outside a school that need the principal, I hoped to uncover even more impressions of the principal's role. To whom is a principal a necessary figure? What do different people expect the principal to provide?

Almost every student identified students, teachers, and parents as people who need the principal. Some students differentiated between "good kids" and "bad kids," both of whom they felt needed the principal. A few students mentioned the janitor, secretary or other staff. The superintendent, the media/community, and visitors, were the least mentioned individuals.

More interesting than the *who* is the *how*. For each group mentioned I probed, "*In what ways* do [students, teachers, etc.] need a principal?" The answers reveal even more student-held beliefs about the principal job.

Students Need the Principal

Most of the students interviewed felt that they and their peers need a principal to provide them with rules and to punish them when they misbehave. The bad kids need the principal to straighten them out, and good kids need the principal to protect them from the bad ones. In fourth-grade words, "Kids need the principal because they don't want other people hurting them." An eighth-grade slant on this theme is that "Students need the principal to get them in trouble if they're bad." As if eighth graders wouldn't get in trouble without a principal to help them!

I expected that students would view the principal role as highly disciplinary; I did *not* expect that students would consider this to be important or necessary. Maybe students have a better understanding of what's good for them than we adults tend to think they do. In addition to behavior issues, students see the principal as someone for them *to look up to, to go to if you're having a problem,* and *to teach them right from wrong.* One student—a seventh grader—even felt that a principal can sometimes be a friend.

Teachers Need the Principal

From a student perspective, teachers need a principal primarily "to tell them what to do." Many students used those exact words. Some were more specific, saying teachers needed the principal "so they know what to teach." One student added that the principal not only tells them (teachers) what to do, but also *how* to do it. The insinuation in many of these students' comments is that teachers wouldn't know what to do if the principal didn't tell them. I got the feeling very few students see teachers as educational experts or decision makers. They are simply employees who do what they're told and rely on the principal to direct them.

Students also recognize that the principal serves in a supervisory capacity over the teachers: *approves what they can and can't do in the classroom, makes sure they're doing their jobs,* and *checks lesson plans.* The teachers need the principal to make decisions, provide answers, and fix things. I believe most teachers and principals would agree that this is one function that principals provide. We might question, however, a tenth grader's belief that "teachers need the principal to keep them from getting out of hand with the students." Then again, I suppose it would depend on the school.

Because most students focus on the disciplinary aspects of the principal role, it is no surprise that many of them perceive that teachers need the principal to help them deal with difficult students. The principal serves as the person to whom teachers "send the students they can't handle," and helps them "figure out what to do with certain students." Some students recognize that the teacher's primary job is to teach, and handling difficult students can interfere with that mission. Thus the principal helps to preserve the quality of the learning environment and makes the teacher's job easier. Of course, other students believe that teachers need the principal to discipline students because the teachers simply aren't able to do it themselves. As you will read in the next section, many students don't think teachers could effectively manage student behavior without a principal in the building.

I was pleasantly surprised to find at least a few students consider the principal–teacher relationship to have a human dimension as well as a professional one. The principal might be someone a teacher goes to "to talk about problems" or "to talk to if you're feeling down." One student used the word "help" when he described how teachers need principals. In other words, teachers need the principal "to *help* them to do their work," not to tell them how to work.

Finally, according to my student sources, teachers look to the principal for their paychecks. One cynical eighth grader stated emphatically, "Teachers need the principal, and there's only one reason for them—to get money!" It might surprise students to know that principals do not write or even sign the payroll checks, nor do they usually control the salary scale. However, I suppose principals indirectly control whether teachers get paid by controlling whether teachers remain employed—though in some cases they have little control over *that*.

Parents Need the Principal

From the student perspective parents need the principal primarily for disciplinary reasons, much as teachers and students do. A fourth grader explains, "The principal could tell them if their kids were being bad or not."

A sixth grader states that parents need the principal "to tell them if their kids have been acting wrong." A ninth grader feels parents need the principal "to figure out ways to get the kids to go to school or stay in school." In addition to merely reporting student behavior, the principal also serves as a sounding board or problem solver. A tenth grader sees the principal as "someone for parents to talk to if they're worried about their child at school." Several others felt that the principal is someone for parents to talk to about their child, mainly with regard to misbehavior.

Students also see principals as a primary means of communication between home and school. They "send notices about what is happening in school," and "let parents know what's going on at school." They also communicate with parents through meetings and conferences. One seventh grader observes that "the principal leads parent involvement in the school—like PTA. He talks about issues with parents in the school." Once again I was pleased to learn that students have an appreciation for a principal's responsibilities beyond the inevitable disciplinary tasks.

Finally, parents need the principal "just to feel their kids are safe," and "to know that the school is going to be good for their kids." Both of these comments came from seventh-grade students; they were the *only* ones to refer to parents' reliance on the principal to provide a safe and healthy place for their children. Ironically, I consider it to be my first responsibility. Nothing else we do matters if the school is not a safe place.

And All the Rest

Those persons rarely identified by students as needing the principal include secretaries, janitors, the librarian, the superintendent, the media/community and visitors. Those who mentioned secretaries and janitors explained that they need principals to tell them what to do and to get them the supplies they need to do their job. The librarian needs the principal "for money," and "to make kids call home about overdue books." The superintendent needs the principal "to report what's going on because he can't be at all the schools at once." The media and community need the principal in order to know what is going on in the school. As one eleventh grade student explained, "When you see someone from the school on TV, it's usually the principal." Finally, visitors in the school need the principal "to show them where to go."

Through my interviews with students I found that they were able to identify many different individuals who need the principal, but the three groups cited most frequently were students, teachers and parents. Students perceive that these individuals need principals for a variety of reasons, not the least of which is behavior management and discipline. Like the previous question, this one revealed the tendency for students to see the principal primarily as a disciplinarian and a manager and rarely as an educational leader. They rarely referred to the principal's role in supporting the teaching and learning processes.

> The most unique response to the question "Who needs the principal?": "The government needs them, too, but I don't know why." (eleventh-grade student)

WHAT DO YOU THINK IT WOULD BE LIKE AT SCHOOL WITHOUT A PRINCIPAL?

This question by far elicited the most surprising, entertaining and alarming responses. Students almost unanimously described a school without a principal as a negative place. In their opinions, nothing would run smoothly, no one would know what to do, safety would be a paramount issue, and students would rule the school.

The student responses to this question are so colorful and descriptive, I am simply going to list a representative sample and save the editorial comments for last. So, what would it be like at school without a principal?

- No one would be in school.
- It would be hard. Maybe some things wouldn't get done.
- Havoc! Mayhem! It wouldn't be fun.
- Each teacher would be different from the others. There would be no basic standards to follow.
- All the teachers would be saying, "I'm better than you are!" The principal keeps them from competing with each other. The principal tells them what to do.

- There would be huge conflicts. I think everyone would learn to hate school—the teachers and the students.
- Conflicts would erupt. Everyone would be angry at everyone else for one reason or another.
- It would be a big mess. Kids would be just goofing off and the teachers would get mad and that would just encourage the kids more.
- There would be much more debates between teachers. There would be no head person to set rules.
- There would probably be more fights and roughhousing.
- Teachers probably wouldn't be as highly skilled. The principal judges that when they hire them.
- Students wouldn't listen to teachers and they would end up taking over really fast. Cuz there's more of us.
- It would be chaos. No leader. All the workers would be fighting over things—including coffee.
- It wouldn't be together at all. It would be all mixed up or crazy.
- It would be BAD. Because the kids would be all hyper and throwing everything around the room and going out in the halls and doing bad stuff.
- It would be like no one helping you. It would be like really confusing. It would be like not a school.
- It would be very miserable. It would be out of control. There would be no disciplinarian for kids to go to when they're in trouble.
- Well—kids would get away with things. All the other kids would be all mean and get in fights.
- Probably everyone would be crabby. There wouldn't be as much education because teachers would have to step out of the classroom to give consequences.
- It would be bad, because if there's no principal then all the kids could do whatever they want—jump around and stuff.
- Bills would pile up. Teachers wouldn't know what to teach.
- It would be crazy and not very organized. Well, there's the teachers, but the principal tells the teachers what to do.

I asked this question because I thought I could learn what students think principals do by having them imagine a school without one. In other words, what tasks or responsibilities would cease to be addressed if the principal were not there to address them? I think their comments are rather revealing.

Students obviously credit the principal with instilling all sense of discipline and order in a school. Without a principal, students would engage in a host of inappropriate and even dangerous behaviors. Teachers would not be able to control them, and students might actually take over the school! What I find surprising about this perception is not that they think student insurrection would ensue, but that they think this would be a bad thing. I truly expected at least some students to consider the lack of a principal a *good* thing—they would be in charge and get to do what they want. But these students found this scenario to be quite frightful.

One might wonder if once again my principal status impacted the students' responses. Perhaps they didn't want to hurt my feelings by saying a school without a principal would be a great thing. I'm going to venture an educated guess and say this wasn't the case. First, considering other responses given by junior high students, if they thought a school without a principal would be heaven on earth, they would have had no qualms about telling me. Second, the students' descriptions are consistent with those generated by the other groups interviewed for this book. I tend to think they reflect a common perception

I was also surprised that students have very little confidence in teachers as disciplinarians. One student mentioned that the students would take over the teachers "because there's more of us." I replied that there is only *one* principal. Why don't they take over now? She replied, "Because we've been taught not to." This tells me that some students don't see teachers as authority figures; it is the threat of the principal's office that keeps students in line. This perception, too, is reiterated in the following chapters.

Another theme that runs throughout these comments is that students see the principal as the one who keeps everything organized. Without the principal in the office, everything would be "mixed up" and "crazy." No one would know what to do. Even the teachers and other staff would argue amongst themselves without the principal to tell them what to do. They would do things their own way and, according to one student, would compete with each other for importance or recognition. The disorganization and unrest caused by the absence of a principal would leave people feeling angry, miserable, and crabby.

In addition to the many comments above, a few students gave less alarming predictions of life without a principal. A high school student replied, "Maybe it would be the same? I don't know. Just don't know the principal job. Never understood it." The eighth-grade student whose first comment was, "Mayhem! Havoc!" qualified her statement by adding, "depending on who the principal is—sometimes it's better when they're gone." A sixth grader figured, "There would probably be less assemblies, not as many flyers—which might be a good thing." With the exception of these three students, however, the general consensus appears to be that a school without a principal would not be successful; it would not be a good place for children or adults.

As a principal I was partly flattered by the student's perception that I alone may be responsible for holding the school together and keeping everyone safe and happy. I was also a little disillusioned to see that many students consider discipline to depend solely on the presence of the principal, as if students treat others with kindness and respect purely out of fear of my wrath. If I read these students perceptions from a teacher point of view, I am offended. Do teachers really have so little competence and authority? Without the "big brother" principal watching and directing their every move, would they cease to know how to teach, how to create respectful classrooms, and how to interact with their peers on a professional level? From the students' point of view, the answer appears to be "yes."

The responses to this question help to reinforce an emerging theme in this chapter. Although students perceive the principal to be many things and to do many things, they primarily see him/her as a disciplinarian and a boss. Without a principal, students would not behave and teachers would not know how to do their jobs.

> The most unique response to the question, "What would it be like at school without a principal?": "I think everybody would be all bruised up." (first-grade student)

IS THERE ANYTHING PRINCIPALS DON'T DO THAT YOU THINK THEY SHOULD?

In my quest to find out what students think principals do, I used many tactics. With this question I hoped that students' perceptions of what principals *don't* do might throw some more light on their assumptions about the job—assumptions based on their own experiences and observations. I predicted that some of the things students think principals *don't* do are actually things that principals already do—the students just don't know it. What I found instead is that this question reveals what students really *want* in a school principal, and what students want can be very useful to those of us who are or hope to be principals. I say this because what most students would like to see principals do is not what you might expect. They don't want us to make recess four hours long, ban homework, or put pizza on the menu every day. These students, for the most part, have higher aspirations for the principal role.

Most of the students I interviewed think that principals should interact more directly with students. They should talk to them, get to know them, and spend more time in the classrooms. A tenth grader sums up what many of them said, "They should be a lot more involved and active with students. I think they should be visible in the school more—don't just observe classes, participate in them too." A sixth grader agrees, "The principal should make friends with the students. They should go around once a week and teach a class for like half an hour just to get an idea of what a teacher's job is like." Students would like to see the principal in the classroom, in the lunchroom, and on the playground. They want the principal to greet students each morning and relate to them on their own level. Most of these comments came from students in the sixth grade and older.

The younger students were more interested in seeing the principal do more in the way of behavior control. A first grader said, "I think the principal should peek into the teachers' rooms to make sure kids aren't doing anything wrong." A fourth grader wants the principal to "come outside and see how everyone's doing out there. People might be doing bad stuff out there." A third-grade student thinks the principal "should make a bus rule about kids kicking other kids out of seats." Students of this age are very focused on the concept of fairness, and it seems they would like the principal to do more toward promoting that. But even these comments suggest a desire for principals to be seen more.

I have two theories about why older students almost unanimously wish for principals to interact with them more, while few younger students brought this up. One explanation is that the concepts of interaction and relating to people are too abstract for the young students. They operate in a concrete world ruled by actions rather than relationships. The other explanation is that perhaps elementary students don't feel student interaction is a deficit with principals and thus they don't identify it as a need. Are elementary principals more involved with students, more visible in their classrooms and throughout the school than middle school or high school principals? I think this is possible. Perhaps the size and structure of many middle schools and high schools make it more difficult for principals to spend positive time with students. Maybe middle school and high school principals don't *want* to or don't think it's important.

Whatever the reason, the students' responses to this question should cause all principals, regardless of level, to reflect upon their relationships with students. Is your interaction with students limited to daily announcements and lecturing kids in your office? When was the last time you stepped into the classroom? When was the last time you taught a lesson, ate lunch in the cafeteria, or spent time on the playground? Do your students see you on a daily basis—I mean other than the ones who are sent to you? Are students ever sent to the office for *good* things; do you encourage that? I think these are important questions, and listening to these student responses has caused me to reflect on these questions daily. Although I feel I have always been very visible in the school and spend time interacting with students, now that I know how important it is to students, I am trying to make this a priority. I challenge my colleagues to do the same.

> The most unique response to the question, "Is there something principals don't do that you think they should?": "I think they should do everything they do now plus what the superintendent does so we wouldn't need one." (eighth-grade student)

BEING A PRINCIPAL IS LIKE BEING . . .

I've heard it said (or perhaps I've read it) that the metaphors we use can illustrate our true beliefs or assumptions about the world. For example, those who say, "Children are the clay and we are the potter," see children as unformed or unfinished beings who need to be made into something worthwhile. They can be made into whatever we, the adults in their life, choose for them to be. Adults, such as teachers or parents, would likely not come right out and describe children as "unformed," but their use of the clay metaphor may reveal their hidden beliefs. This is just a theory, mind you. Applying metaphors, such as describing children as clay, does not entail that the object to which a metaphor is applied is conceptually similar to the metaphorical object itself. Indeed, there are many more dissimilarities than similarities between clay and children. However, an intuited, if not fully articulated, similarity between the likened items must have led to applying the metaphor.

I attempted to use a related technique to unearth children's underlying beliefs about the principal role. In this case I went for a simile rather than a metaphor. As children compare being a principal to being something else, I feel they reveal some of the ideas they have about what principals do. If one thing is like another it means they share some common features and/or functions. So let's find out what children compare to principals.

About a fourth of the students said being a principal is like being the boss or manager of a business. They "have to keep everything running smoothly," and "they have to do the same kinds of work—the budgets, the paperwork, get the paychecks to workers." Both principals and business managers have to do a lot of work, and they are responsible for the entire organization, including the employees. A third-grade student said, "Being a principal is like being a manager because you're sort of owning kids for a length of time." No hidden assumptions here!

Other common similes emerged. To some students, principals are like teachers. They both: *work in schools, do a lot of work,* and *tell kids what needs to be done.* The teacher is the head of the classroom in the same way that the principal is the head of the school. Several students compared being a principal to being the president. A tenth grader's explanation will hit home for many principals: "Being a principal is like being the president because everyone expects you to solve their problem now, but you can only do one thing at a time." A seventh grader recognized that while both the president and a principal have responsible positions, they both have a lot of people around them to help. An equal number of students compared being a principal to being a parent. Like principals, parents "have to make sure their kids are behaving," and "they sometimes yell at you." Both parents and principals have to work a lot and they "sign bills."

All other student comparisons fall in the "single mention" category. Individual students replied that being a principal is like being: *a mayor, a priest, a lawyer* and *a coach.* A kindergarten student said that being a principal is like being "my dad—because he works a lot." A principal is often said to wear many hats, and these students' responses support that analogy.

Do these comparisons teach us anything about students' perceptions of the principal role? I don't think they reveal any heretofore hidden assumptions. Like the previous questions, this comparison question suggests that students recognize the managerial role of the principal. Once again, students don't make a strong connection between the principal's job and the educational process. Even when principals were compared to teachers, the reasons had to with the amount of work they both do, not the type. *Unlike* the responses to the other questions, however, these comparisons downplayed the disciplinary aspects of the principal job. Most of the comparisons and their explanations focused on keeping an organization running smoothly and being in charge. Happily, none of these students compared being a principal to being a prison warden, but I suspect there are students for whom this perception exists.

> The most unique response to the question, "Being a principal is like being...": "The owner of a grocery store—because you never see the owner of the grocery store, and when you do he's not doing anything." (recent graduate)

WHY DO YOU THINK PEOPLE CHOOSE TO BECOME PRINCIPALS?

Once again, my student sources surprised me. The reasons they gave for a person choosing this career are overwhelmingly positive and altruistic. Of the students interviewed, seventy-four percent cited liking students or a desire to help students as reasons people choose to be a principal. Some elaborated by saying things such as "they like helping kids learn what's necessary for life," or "they enjoy helping kids get through school and through life." Many of these students are the same ones who focused on the disciplinary and managerial aspects of the principal role. Despite this perception, they believe that principals like kids and helping them is one of their primary goals.

Of course there were some of the expected responses to this question. Some students think people choose to be principals because they like bossing kids or people or because they want to make a lot of money. A few suggested that people become principals because they are tired of teaching, but want to still work in schools or "they want a higher rank." These are certainly all reasons some people choose to move into the principal position, though not the most admirable ones. I smiled at one student's response: "Because they like to be a teacher, but they want to walk around the school."

What we can learn from students' responses to this question is that most students think that principals care about them; they like them and want to help them. These aren't pure guesses. These students must see their principals doing things that demonstrate an interest in the welfare of children. These children must be able to conclude that even when principals discipline them or set rules they are doing so for the good of the students. Very few of the children saw the principal role as one of pure power or financial gain.

If you are a principal you might wonder, do my students feel the same? How do I demonstrate my mission or my goals to my students? Do they see me as someone whose first concern is their well being, or as a person who values power and personal gain? A final, and critical, question I pose to principals is, what are your reasons for becoming a principal? Have you chosen this path for the students or for yourself? Your answer to this question has major implications for you and for the people you are entrusted to serve.

The most unique response to the question, "Why do you think people choose to become principals?": "Free coffee." (eighth-grade student)

SO, WOULD YOU WANT TO BE A PRINCIPAL?

I'm not sure what I expected from students with regard to this question. Before starting the interviews, I don't know if I had a prediction about whether most would or would not want this job. What I found is that most of them don't—seventy-one percent to be more specific. But it's not whether or not students would want to be a principal that's significant, it's their reasoning that provides insight into their perceptions of the principal role.

The students who would not want to be principals feel that way because they perceive aspects of the job that are unappealing to them. Some see the job as involving too much work or stress. They also recognize that principals have to do some unpleasant things. A fourth-grade student notes that "you have to be strict." A sixth grader responds negatively because "I wouldn't want to fire teachers—or hire them." An eleventh-grade student sees the job as "too many people complaining to me." These students obviously recognize that the principal job involves more than walking around the halls, telling people what to do, and drinking free coffee. They appreciate the heavy workload and the fact that principals deal with difficult and unpleasant situations.

Those who answered positively to this question had mainly admirable reasons for doing so. The most heart-warming response was, "Seeing what you do looks like a fun job." Another stated that, "It would probably make you feel good about what you do." Only one gave a not-so-admirable reason: "Maybe for the high pay and summers off." I'm not so naïve as to think this is not a reason some people aspire to the principalship. I can only hope it's an exception to the rule.

The foregoing question about possibly becoming a principal reveals that most students do not have glorified conceptions of the principal job. They recognize both the physical and emotional challenges of being the leader in a school. They also recognize the non-tangible rewards of doing work that is worthwhile and of service to others. And, yes, some of them recognize the perks! From this one question I learned that at least some students have a fairly good understanding of the negative and positive aspects of being a principal.

The most unique response to the question, "So, would you want to be a principal?": "Sure—just doesn't look like a hard job." (high school student)

SOME CONCLUDING THOUGHTS ON WHAT STUDENTS THINK PRINCIPALS DO

While students shared many ideas about what principals do, it is obvious that their most prominent perception of the role is that of a disciplinarian. A principal not only makes up rules, s/he enforces rules and doles out punishments. This is hardly a misconception. Though many of us may like to think of ourselves as so much more than that, the truth of the matter is most principals spend a lot of time handling issues related to student behaviors. When teachers face discipline issues they cannot resolve, the students are sent to the principal. The principal notifies parents of severe or recurring misbehaviors, implements strategies for dealing with those misbehaviors, and determines appropriate consequences based on school policies. This is especially true in smaller or medium-sized schools. In larger schools, managing student behavior is often relegated to the assistant principal, the dean of students, or a similar role. But even in those schools, the principal still serves as the highest authority in behavior matters, especially in cases that lead to suspension or expulsion.

I am not surprised or even dissatisfied that students perceive me as someone concerned with and involved in behavior management. What concerns me is that some students put such emphasis on this role. It is not my goal to "strike fear in the hearts of men (or children)." I do not want a visit to the principal's office to be analogous to a trip to the gallows. Although I want students to know I have high expectations for respectful and responsible behavior, I don't want them to think my goal each day is to catch students being bad.

So what might principals do to expand upon the disciplinarian perception? One suggestion is that principals could foster a more positive perception by focusing as much on good behavior as they do on inappropriate behavior. I know I'm not the first principal to have this revelation. I have heard or read of strategies employed by principals to encourage good choices and kind acts. First of all, we can publicly acknowledge students who display good behaviors when we see them in the hall, in the lunchroom or on the playground. Principals can also encourage teachers and other staff members to send students to the principal for good reasons—because they helped or stood up for a classmate in need, because they volunteered to pick up litter on the playground, because they wrote a wonderful poem or got a good grade on their science test.

How many principals have called a parent (or had a student call a parent) to report misbehavior or missing work? This can be an effective deterrent for students whose parents support school discipline measures. Might it not be an equally motivating factor to call a parent and say, "Your child was sent to the office because he showed compassion for another student today," or "This is the principal calling to let you know your child wrote a beautiful essay in English class"? Perhaps some students would be able to say, "I *got* to go to the principal's office today," instead of "I *had* to go to the principal's office today."

The other pattern of thinking that strikes me as significant is students' apparent lack of confidence in their teachers. They seem to think that teachers would not know how or what to teach without principals to tell them. Students also tend to see the teacher as a fairly insignificant authority figure. If teachers didn't have the safety net of the principal's office, student behavior would be out of control. I'm betting this perception extends to other staff like the playground supervisor, the secretary or the librarian. The question I have for my colleagues and myself is, how do we address this phenomenon if it exists in our school? How can principals empower faculty and staff in the eyes of students so that their expertise is valued and their position respected?

Although my research for this chapter unearthed some ideas that caused dismay, I was also pleasantly surprised by the scope and variety of many students' perceptions. Students above the age of eight or nine exhibit an awareness and appreciation of many aspects of the principal role. Even when their perceptions seem narrow or limited, the students are not to blame. Their perceptions are based on their experiences and observations. Students tend to see principals as managers and disciplinarians mainly because that is the historical and social construction of the role in most schools. Only in the past decade or so have the concepts of leadership and service been associated with the role of the principal, and then only in emerging philosophies and literature. It will take some time before these concepts filter down from theory to practice.

Chapter Three

What Parents Think Principals Do

INTRODUCTION

The viewpoints discussed in this chapter reflect those of parents who currently have children in schools. I sought the perceptions of those for whom the parent-principal relationship is both immediate and relevant. Those parents whose children are grown are included in the community chapter. I did not interview any parents from my own school setting. I asked the same questions of parents that I did of students, but once again I do not share responses to all of the questions, only those I feel are most indicative of the parent perspective.

WHAT IS A PRINCIPAL?

Parent definitions are similar to those of students. The principal of a school is:

- the head person
- in charge
- the top person
- a leader
- the person responsible for administering a school
- the big cheese

The principal is primarily a boss who takes charge of and oversees everyone and everything in a school. Less popular definitions include:

coordinator, role model, friend. Only one parent referred to the principal as a disciplinarian, which differs from the student focus. This perception surfaces through other questions, however.

> The most unique response to the question, "What is a principal?": "The ultimate god!"

WHAT DO PRINCIPALS DO?

Parents provided more varied responses to this question than students. A few said they had no idea or honestly didn't know, but with probing they were able to offer a list of ideas. I could tell that many parents felt self-conscious about their knowledge of the job, as their responses were often preceded by phrases like, "I'm only guessing..." or "I imagine..." Their uneasiness was understandable considering they all know I am a principal. I am sure some of them felt they were offending me by not knowing more about what I do.

Parents identified the obvious tasks performed by principals—disciplining students, solving problems, communicating with everyone, overseeing teachers and students, and doing paperwork. Like students, parents observe the principal performing many managerial and disciplinary tasks. Not surprisingly, parents referred more frequently than students to financial responsibilities—managing a budget and seeking additional funding. Only three parents identified the principal's role in teaching and learning, referring to the development and supervision of curriculum and the evaluation of teacher effectiveness.

Several parents shared some uncomplimentary perceptions of the principal role. For example:

- They're always busy—you can't get in to see them.
- They take longer breaks than anyone else.
- They walk down the hall and yell at you.
- My son's principal sits back, reclined in a chair reading magazines or something. That's about all I've seen him do.

- They're all administrative fluff as far as I'm concerned.
- Most of the time they're hardly ever seen.

These parents are likely reflecting on their experiences with specific principals—either from their pasts as students or their current role as a parents. Their comments illustrate how one particular situation or one particular person can influence one's overall perception. The memory of one bad apple can affect your evaluation of the whole bunch. This phenomenon is significant to me as a principal. If a parent appears wary of my intentions or treats me less than warmly, it may be due to my own actions, or it may be due to that parent's past experience with another principal. Part of the principal's job may be to counteract the negative school experiences parents carry with them.

> The most unique response to the question, "What do principals do?": "Did I say they get longer breaks than anyone else?"

WHY DOES A SCHOOL NEED A PRINCIPAL?

Although some of the parent responses to the previous questions were less than complimentary, every parent agreed that a school needs a principal. The most common reason given is that "somebody needs to be in charge." Parents see the need for a boss who supervises all the operations in a school, who can answer questions, and who can make final decisions. The principal is also needed because they have knowledge about legal issues and policies that others do not. Even the parent who considered principals to be "administrative fluff" felt that "administratively they need somebody at the top—to pass on things to those above." A principal is the person who holds everyone else accountable in the school.

One parent mentioned that a principal is needed because "there's an air when the principal is in the building, like the students just know." Another agreed, saying, "Kids are all scared. They don't want to see the principal." From this perspective, the knowledge that a principal is present serves as a preventative measure—and not only with students.

Another parent suggested that the principal keeps the teachers in line. "Otherwise the teachers would get away with not keeping up—may not even teach class!"

Two other responses to this question bear mentioning. One parent suggested that whether or not a school needs a principal depends on the size of the school. This response struck a chord with me because in the midst of my interviewing I quickly discerned that school size factors into many of my questions (more on that in the final chapter). This same parent makes another interesting point about the need for a principal: "You need somebody to act in that capacity, whether or not it's termed 'principal.'" It isn't necessarily a principal that a school needs, but a *person* who is in charge and oversees all others. The title is not as important as the job description.

> The most unique response to the question, "Why does a school need a principal?": "Somebody should be there—to sit up on the throne like Queen Elizabeth."

WHO NEEDS THE PRINCIPAL?

As with the students, I asked parents to identify specific groups of people within or outside a school that need the principal, hoping to uncover even more impressions of the principal's role. They identified the same groups that students did: students, parents, teachers, and other staff.

Parents Need the Principal

The number one reason parents need a principal is for problem solving. Parents need the principal "to contact if they don't like the way something is going at school," or "if they have a child who isn't doing well." Parents see the principal as the "go-to person" for problems, concerns, questions, and information. It is important to parents that there be somebody they can talk to besides the teacher—especially if the problem *is* the teacher.

A secondary need from the parent point of view is the need to have communication between home and school, and the principal is primarily responsible for that. The principal keeps parents informed about how their child is doing at school, both academically and behaviorally. The principal also informs parents of "what goes on at school and at the district level." Parents see the principal as the "go-to" information person, the one who knows what is going on at all times. One parent admitted, "It's just comforting to me to know that the principal is there." As a principal, it's just comforting to me to know that somebody cares that I'm there!

Teachers Need the Principal

Parents assume that teachers need the principal mainly to help with problem students. As one parent put it, "to take care of that bad apple in class instead of them having to do it." Some parents also believe teachers need the principal to answer questions—about curriculum, about students, and about "what they need to do." The principal provides the teachers with guidance and support. Two parents recognized that teachers might need the principal to help when they have problems with another teacher, and two others referred to problems with a difficult parent.

Only one parent mentioned that teachers need the principal for recognition. "Somebody's gotta walk up and say, 'Gee, you're doing a hot job!'" Another suggested that the principal could "buy 'em lunch once in a while." None of the other parents recognized that teachers might look to the principal for a pat on the back or words of encouragement. As a principal, I believe this is a very important part of the principal–teacher relationship. Teachers are isolated from other adults most of the time and often question their effectiveness in the classroom (at least the good ones do). Like anyone, they need to be told what they do well as often as they are told what to improve.

Students Need the Principal

I expected parents would feel that students need the principal to serve as an authority figure and a deterrent to misbehavior. Two parents reiterated what many students said in the last chapter, "There is a different level of respect that a student has for the principal than for a teacher," and "Teachers aren't always looked at as an ultimate authority." Is it just students who discount the authority of teachers, or do parents as well? Might parents somehow unconsciously reinforce this student perception?

Several parents think that students need the principal to help them when they have a problem with a teacher. They need to know someone else is there, a "hierarchy" of command. The principal is also a person they can go to with other problems, including problems at home. Parents did not specify any educational reasons why students might need the principal.

Other Staff Need the Principal

Only a few parents referred to other staff. Specifically they mentioned secretaries and custodians, who need the principal to "give them things to do" and to hold them accountable—"Are you doing your job?" For them the principal is also the "go-to person" for problems and answers. One astute parent said the secretary needs the principal "in order to have a job."

> The most unique response to the question, "Who needs the principal?": "Teachers need the principal more than the kids do. They've got enough on their plate; they don't need to be where the buck stops."

WHAT DO YOU THINK IT WOULD BE LIKE AT SCHOOL WITHOUT A PRINCIPAL?

Parents aren't quite as alarmed at this prospect as students are, but they certainly are not in favor of the idea. The most extreme answer to this question was, "Chaos." Six parents used that particular term. Similar extreme answers include: *a free-for-all, way big problems, a mess* and *it would fall apart.* Some parents were more moderately concerned, using terms like: *potential chaos, disorganized,* and *more complicated.* One parent felt that a school could "somewhat function without a principal," but teachers would have to spend more time on discipline and less on teaching. Another optimistic parent felt that a team model could be an alternate source of leadership, though he added, "if the teams don't work well together, then there would be chaos."

While students are mostly concerned with disciplinary chaos, parents are more concerned with organizational chaos. They feel that without a principal everybody would be doing their own thing. One parent explains, "Faculty would be doing what they think is right or best, and I don't think that would be good." Another states, "I think you would see a lot more variance in teaching methods. Without a principal teachers would take off on a tangent and do their own thing." A baby boomer parent worried that "it would be like a commune—people would be going different ways. There would be no one to hold the flock together." The general consensus appears to be that principals provide the direction for a school. They set standards and uphold uniform expectations for behavior, teaching, and decision making.

Although parents don't think students would take over the school without a principal, they do think that student behavior would deteriorate. One concerned parent warned, "Somebody's got to be in charge of the kids." And another: "I think the kids would really not be good to the teachers, because there's no one else they have to answer to." Like the students, parents feel that the principal provides a necessary level of authority that acts as a deterrent to misbehavior. As a principal, I can attest to the fact that this "positional power" exists. Teachers have told me more than once, "They're so different when you're here," or "Nothing ever goes wrong when you're in the lunchroom." The age-old threat to send a student to the principal's office usually puts an end to most classroom misbehaviors. I know that some teachers and staff members are nervous when I'm out of the building because if something goes wrong there will be no one to take care of it. Of course, someone *will* take care of it, but they would certainly rather it was me!

I'm a little surprised that parents think the lack of a principal would be so critical to the school environment. I expected them to have more faith than students in the competency of teachers. Although the prediction of chaos serves as job security for my principal colleagues and me, I'm disconcerted that parents put so much faith in one role and so little faith in the others. I'm beginning to see that someone needs to write a book about what people think teachers do. Just a thought.

> The most unique response to the question, "What do you think it would be like at school without a principal?": "Anarchy."

WHY DO YOU THINK PEOPLE CHOOSE TO BECOME PRINCIPALS?

I asked this question because I hoped parents' ideas of underlying motives might shed light on their perceptions of the principal role, or at least their perceptions of the types of people who fulfill that role. Do parents consider principals to be altruistic, dedicated, ambitious, greedy, or indifferent? Do principals seek to lead or control or merely retire? Might parents' answers to those questions affect their views of what principals do?

All the parents I interviewed provided more than one reason people become principals. I am happy to report that most parents think people choose to be principals for non-selfish reasons. Principals are thought to have leadership tendencies and a desire to improve education. Some sample responses to this question are:

- They feel they can make a difference—impact school policies that would help kids.
- To make some positive changes.
- They really think that they may be able to do some good and affect students' education.
- Because they love education and they want the students to have an appreciation for education and learning.
- They're born leaders.

The second most popular answer is less admirable, but not untrue. Many parents think people move into the principal position in order to get out of the classroom. In the words of one parent, "Some want to be principals for the sheer fact that 'I've taught for this many years and it's time for a change.'" Others agree that some aspiring principals are either tired of teaching or burned out. A related reason identified by two parents is some principals seek to have more influence in the school than they can as teachers.

Three reasons share the third place spot for this question. People choose to become principals because they like kids, to make more money, and to move up the career ladder. They are interested in both helping students and bettering themselves. One parent surmises, "It's more prestigious to be a principal—sounds good to say you're a principal." Similarly, "Ego" was cited by one parent as the reason some choose the job.

I would say that parents have a fairly good perception of the reasons people become principals. They all identified a variety of reasons, not just one. I would venture to guess that all of their reasons are accurate for at least some principals. Yes, some people are looking for a better salary or a higher position. Some are tired of teaching or in need of a change. Some are change agents who seek to have an influence on the way schools run. Some love children and want to create a better place for them. And some are born leaders. It is likely that one's reasons for becoming a principal are apparent to others, and thus affect the way others perceive you and the role in general.

> The most unique response to the question, "Why do you think people choose to become principals?": "Because they're out of their minds!"

WHAT DO YOU THINK WOULD BE HARDEST ABOUT THE JOB?

A person cannot answer this question without revealing one's ideas of what a principal does. Parents revealed to me that they consider the principal job to involve a lot of problems. Some think that "handling problem children" would be the hardest part of the job, while others think "dealing with the parents of problem children" would offer the most challenge. The number of parents who identified parents as a difficulty surprised me. Some are especially critical of parents who do not support the school's authority or who will not admit that "their child can do anything wrong." Some parents simply referred to problems in general. "It would be difficult handling all the problems. There's always going to be somebody calling to complain."

Another common response involves dealing with personnel issues. Parents think it would be difficult to "reprimand a faculty member" or fire somebody. It would be hard to work with "a teacher who is unhappy with her job." Dealing with unions and tenure were also identified as difficult areas, especially when they prevent a principal from terminating an ineffective teacher.

Parents also see principals being challenged by the sheer scope of the role. It would be difficult "balancing everything and keeping the ship afloat." One parent painted a rather grim picture of what principals face: "It would be difficult to maintain a calm attitude. You've got teachers screaming and yelling because they want this or that. You've got parents screaming and yelling because the teacher didn't do whatever. And then you've got the upper administration telling you to get more work out of the teachers." While I don't see a lot screaming and yelling by teachers and parents, I certainly agree that principals are pulled in many different directions and are sometimes expected to address competing expectations. In fact, many principals struggle with the enormity of this challenge. How can you possibly meet everybody's expectations when they so often contradict each other?

Two parents touched on what I consider to be a difficult aspect of the job—dealing with the financial side of education. One parent stated that a major difficulty would be "wanting to provide services, but having no money." I am often disillusioned by the fact that money rules so much of what we do. It is difficult to tell a parent or a teacher that we can't provide an opportunity for students because it isn't in the budget. In a perfect world money should not limit our goals for education or our services for children, but the stark reality is it often does.

This question revealed to me that parents recognize the principal job is often consumed with problem solving and listening to complaints. Though principals might have other items on their agenda—long-term planning, improving teaching and learning, building partnerships in the community—these loftier goals must often take a back seat to more immediate, problem-ridden issues. The lesson for principals and aspiring principals is, if you don't like problem solving and prefer to avoid conflict, you may want to pursue another career.

It is reassuring to know that most parents recognize the problems principals face and the factors that often dictate or limit our actions. Some principals may think parents don't adequately appreciate their role, but I think a lot of them do. One parent admitted, "In a lot of ways it's gotta be a thankless job." Principals may sometimes feel that way, but the fact that some parents recognize this possibility means it isn't necessarily so.

> The most unique response to the question, "What do you think would be hardest about the job?": "I don't know. They get up, they go to work, they sit at a desk and do God knows what."

SO, WOULD YOU WANT TO BE A PRINCIPAL?

Most parents—seventy-five percent—answered "no" to this question, some with undisguised emotion. Their reasons are typical: *too much responsibility, too busy, no appreciation, don't like to make the big decisions,* and *too hard to please everybody.* These parents do not consider themselves to possess either the patience or the energy to handle all that being a principal entails. Two parents referred to the challenge of working with students. One mother explains, "You have to be a special person. First, you have to be a teacher, and I have no patience to do that. I can barely get through my forty-minute Sunday school lesson each week." Another mother admits, "A mass number of children would drive me insane by the end of the day." These parents do not consider the principal job to be an easy one; nor do they consider the rewards or perks to outweigh the challenges.

The few parents who expressed an interest in being a principal like the idea of working with children and helping people. One is attracted to the business aspects of the job—organizing and communicating. She even likes "working with budgets." (Sign her up for principal training!) One father said he could imagine being a principal because "I'm a dictating, ego-bent, hell-raising, anti-bureaucrat who would raise cane and take names." I'm not sure this gentleman has a true desire to be a principal, but he certainly has some strong feelings about the job. Sure, there's a degree of facetiousness in his response, but also a measure of dissatisfaction with the current structure of the principal role. He made it clear to me that the job description for principals is both limiting and outdated.

Most parents, like students, do not want to be principals. The job appears too demanding and too stressful, the rewards too small. Does that mean these parents admire people who aspire to this challenging role? Or do they merely think, as one parent suggested, that principals are crazy? To what extent do principals meet parents' expectations? Responses to the next two questions offer some insight.

> The most unique response to the question, "So, would you want to be a principal?": "I could imagine being a principal—because I'm a dictating, egobent, hell-raising anti-bureaucrat who would raise cane and take names!"

WHO IS YOUR FAVORITE PRINCIPAL?

I expanded on this question by asking parents to think of all the principals they have known, either as children or adults, and tell me about the one for whom they have the highest regard. Most parents identified a principal they have known through their children's school experience, mainly because they either could not remember the principals from their own youth or their recollections were highly negative: "The others were so bad, or I never knew them." And, "The other principals I don't really remember—except for the scary one!"

When parents described their favorite principals, a common characteristic became very clear. Parents like and admire a principal who is visible and involved. The following responses illustrate the significance of this attribute:

- He was always around the kids.
- You always saw her; she was never hiding in her office. She really knew the kids.
- He was rarely at his desk, always with the kids. In the classrooms, halls, library.
- I admire his involvement—he's always there for every event. He knows your name and says hi when he sees you.
- He had an open door policy, was out in the hallway. He was not a mysterious person behind the door. Not someone to be feared.

These responses are so similar one might think they all came from the same person, but each response reflects a different parent's account of his/her favorite principal—and these are only a few of many. Parents truly value a principal who is seen often and who is directly involved with both students and parents. They prefer to see the principal out of the office than it. The following section takes an even closer look at what parents would like to see principals do.

> The most unique response to the question, "Who is your favorite principal?": "I have nothing bad to say about any of them—nothing good either."

IS THERE ANYTHING PRINCIPALS DON'T DO THAT YOU THINK THEY SHOULD?

A few generous souls said no, principals do enough already. Most had some ideas of what they would like to see principals do. In some cases the parent explained, it isn't that the principal doesn't do this, they just need to do it *more*. As one might expect from the previous section, parents would like to see principals have more student contact. They would like to see principals "connect with students more" and "get to know kids better." This includes spending more time in the halls, the lunchroom, and on the playground. Parents would also like to see principals teach now and then, perhaps serve as a substitute for absent teachers. There are principals who do this. For most, however, it is either inconceivable, given their workload, or it simply doesn't appeal to them. If one became a principal to escape the classroom, then substitute teaching would not be high on the list of things to do.

In addition to connecting with students, principals should socialize more with parents and teachers. One parent thinks they "should be seen more on a human level." Another wants them to "be seen more by the public—be more community oriented." One parent suggestion is for principals to "float through the halls during conferences to chat with parents." Many principals do these things, but from the perspective of these parents, not enough of them do—or they don't do it enough.

A principal looking to earn the respect and admiration of parents would do well to step out of the office on a regular basis, interact with people (especially students), and basically just be seen. So who is going to write that district report, return those phone calls, and approve those purchase orders? That's one of the challenges of the principal's job—figuring out how to develop strong relationships without neglecting the stuff on your desk. Principals who strive to balance the human dimensions of leadership with all the other tasks, do not leave the building when the last bus rolls away from the curb; that's when they finally turn to all the stuff they never got to during the school day.

The most unique response to the question, "Is there anything principals don't do that you think they should?": "Some kind of poster or a list on the wall of what a principal does might be enlightening."

WHAT DO YOU THINK PEOPLE LEARN ABOUT IN PRINCIPAL SCHOOL?

This was my final question. I thought if people could identify the skills and knowledge taught in a principal training program, their responses would reveal more of their perceptions of the principal job. The first revelation is that some parents do not realize that the principalship requires additional training. Some initial responses were, "I didn't know there was a principal school," or "I'm pretty sure there isn't one." I explained that it is not really called "principal school," but there are requirements for additional schooling and licensure. Even then, some were surprised. "You have to take classes for that?" And, "I thought it was just a matter of getting enough experience in schools."

The parents I interviewed had a few ideas, but most of them were hard-pressed to come up with more than two or three. The most popular answer was "psychology," which translates into knowing how to deal with people of many ages and personalities. Other common topics include budget and finance, management skills, law, and leadership training. Only one person mentioned issues related to personnel management. Another hopes principal interns learn about compassion. That sums up parent perceptions of what principal training programs provide.

Although the parents identified typical topics found in principal training programs, I was most struck by what they omitted. They did not mention training in the supervision and evaluation of staff, curriculum development, communication skills or public relations. Previous responses showed that parents are not unaware of these aspects of the role. However, it seems they are not the most *significant* aspects of the role from the parent point of view. Or perhaps parents think training in these areas is not necessary, because they are covered in teacher training programs. Regardless of what parents did or did not identify as topics for principal school, the significant revelation to me is that few parents realize the educational requirements for the position. Might parents change their views of the principal role if they were to know it requires multiple degrees and state licensure? My research does not answer that question, but it is worth considering.

> The most unique response to the question, "What do you think people learn about in principal school?": "When not to roll your eyes at a parent; how not to swear."

SOME CONCLUDING THOUGHTS ON WHAT PARENTS THINK PRINCIPALS DO

Overall, parents have a fairly good understanding of the principal role. They see the principal doing many different things for many different people. One aspect of the job that most parents don't grasp is the principal's role as an instructional leader. Principals are not just concerned with how students behave, but with how well they are learning. Principals are also responsible for helping to improve teachers' classroom practice. They plan staff development activities, encourage the reading of professional literature, and observe teachers in the classroom. Some of the other elements parents and other groups failed to mention about the principalship will be discussed in the final chapter.

I would like to make two points about parents' perceptions of principals. First, the assumptions parents possess about the type of people principals are and the type of work they do is influenced by the specific principals they have known. Parents who have had good experiences with principals—their own or their children's—have fairly positive perceptions of principals in general. Those who have known one or two ineffective principals have developed negative or even cynical perceptions. This is illustrated by parents who made comments like, "They're all administrative fluff," "They get up, they go to work, they sit at their desk," and "They walk down the hall and yell at you." These parents are probably remembering principals they have encountered. If the principals parents have seen or known appear lazy, mean or ineffective, they might assume that others are as well.

Principals need to understand that parents carry some preconceptions about the role based on previous experiences, both good and bad. I might have to live up to the standards set by a previous principal. A parent may have loved their child's former principal because she was so personable and involved; thus I am expected to exhibit the same characteristics. On the other hand, a parent may harbor bad feelings and distrust from a previous relationship with a principal. Those negative feelings may be transferred to me because I hold the same position. As principals, we need to recognize that we are often called to either fill someone else's shoes or to counteract the effects of negative memories.

On a related plane, I have also noticed that to parents we are sometimes not individuals, we are the position. I can't recall how many times I have called a parent and heard them whisper to their child, "Sh! It's the principal!" As if I didn't have a name. A principal by any other name would be the same, so to speak. I suppose it's just the nature of the role. It may help principals to know that when you put on the principal's hat, it is sort of a collective hat, shared and shaped by all the others who came before you. If you're lucky, you can adjust yourself to its many forms and still preserve your integrity.

The second point relates to a student perception—specifically students' apparent disregard for teachers as authority figures and their lack of confidence in teachers' professional competency. In this chapter, parents confirmed that students do not have the same respect for teachers that they do for principals. I would venture to guess that it's not just the students, but many parents as well. Might parents either consciously or unconsciously reinforce students' opinions of teachers? After all, parents are influenced by their own childhood perceptions of principals, which they tend to pass down to their children.

This seems like a vicious circle. Should principals be concerned about it? Is there a way to empower teachers in the eyes of others so that their effectiveness is not assumed to depend entirely upon the principal's presence? Maybe we need to start by empowering the teachers first in their own eyes. Have they become too dependent upon the principal to solve problems and provide answers, and has this dependence become apparent to others? I'm not suggesting principals withdraw support and assistance. I'm only suggesting we might help teachers develop more confidence in themselves to know things and handle conflicts. Principals can still be there for them, but in a less directive role. The next chapter should help reveal whether teachers' effectiveness relies as strongly on the principal as students and parents believe.

Chapter Four

What Teachers Think Principals Do

INTRODUCTION

Since teachers work so closely with principals on a professional level, one would expect they have a better understanding of the principal's role than either students or parents. I believe the perceptions shared in this chapter support that prediction, but even teachers expressed some uncertainty about what principals do: "I know they do a lot, and I probably don't know all of it."

I interviewed teachers from kindergarten to high school in a variety of public and private school settings. The smallest school has a staff of twelve, the largest a staff of over one hundred. Their experience ranges from a first-year teacher to a thirty-year veteran.

WHAT IS A PRINCIPAL?

Teachers' definitions differ greatly from those of students and parents. A majority used the term "leader" or "somebody who leads the school." Only one teacher used the term "manager" and none said, "boss" or "administrator." Teachers perceive principals to fill a leadership role more than a managerial role. Though teachers fall below principals on the organizational flow chart, they see the principal not as someone who is in charge of them, but as someone who helps them. This is exemplified in the use of terms like: *colleague, educator, mentor, facilitator,* and *the go-to person.* The responses to this one question suggest that the principal–teacher relationship is less autocratic than students and parents perceive.

WHAT DO PRINCIPALS DO?

Teachers have a good understanding of what principals do. Their combined responses cover most of the tasks and responsibilities performed by principals. In addition to listing specific items, many of the teachers remarked that the principal is responsible for "everything." They have to be everywhere, communicate with everyone, and make sure everything gets done.

Handling student behavior issues and managing a budget were identified most often. This seems to suggest that teachers, like students and parents, consider the principal role to be primarily a disciplinary and managerial one. Yet other responsibilities received almost as many mentions: *communicating with parents, observing and evaluating staff, supporting and leading staff,* and *planning and attending meetings.* Teachers also recognize curriculum management and staff development as primary functions of the school principal. As one would expect, teachers are more aware of the role principals play in the teaching and learning process.

Teachers mentioned several principal responsibilities that received little or no mention by the students and parents. Most teachers perceive the principal's role in connecting the school to the district and state educational systems. The principal "relays information from the district or state to teachers" and "reports to the superintendent." Teachers see the principal as someone who provides advice and guidance as they need it. They look to the principal for support, not to be told what to do.

Staff development is a term common to educators, but less known or ambiguous to those outside the field, which is why it was not referred to by students and parents. Staff development includes workshops, inservice training, conferences, coursework, and professional literature, all aimed at increasing the teachers' knowledge base and teaching skills. The principal is the person who most often plans or schedules staff development activities. Staff development is also required for licensure renewal, so teachers see it as an important function of the principal role.

I was surprised that only one teacher referred to paperwork or office work as something principals do. One reason may be that teachers were able to identify specific tasks that fall into that category (reports, budgets) and thus did not need to resort to the general term. Another possible explanation is that the paperwork aspect of the principal job is as mysterious to teachers as it is to others. I know much of it was unknown to me until I was required to do it—and *I* went to principal school!

> The most unique response to the question "What do principals do?": "They're always working on something; I just don't know what it is."

WHY DOES A SCHOOL NEED A PRINCIPAL?

All of the teachers interviewed feel that a school needs a principal. From the teacher perspective, principals provide the "big picture" focus that no one else can. They coordinate everything and "keep the whole school connected." Principals are the ones who know what everyone else needs to be doing in the school, and they provide the leadership that makes everyone's job easier. Reflecting on this question, one high school teacher admits, "I can't imagine our building operating without a principal." Another remarks, "Good schools have good principals." If you are a principal who feels under-appreciated by the teaching staff, you may find some inspiration in this chapter.

Principals are also needed for decision making. As one teacher said, "When you lead by committee, nothing gets done." Another states that "Sometimes a decision needs to be made in an efficient way; somebody has to do that." The general feeling among teachers is there needs to be *one* person who has the final say about things. There needs to be one leader, one person in charge of everyone and everything.

Two teachers think the school needs a principal to serve as a higher authority figure for students, but more teachers referred to the role principals fulfill for teachers. It's human nature to have a what's-in-it-for-me focus, and teachers are no different. They need principals to "oversee what we do" and "provide advice on how to handle problems." Teachers also recognize that the principal does things teachers might otherwise have to do. "There are so many things that go on in a school; it would get in the way of teaching if teachers had to handle everything." Another teacher concurs, "There is no way teachers would have time to be in touch with the next level [of administration]."

With the next question, teachers were given the opportunity to reflect further on why *they* need the principal, but I also pushed them to consider others in the school.

> The most unique response to the question "Does a school need a principal?": "Some of the principals I've known? Probably not."

WHO NEEDS THE PRINCIPAL?

Teachers identified teachers, parents, students and staff as persons who need a principal, and with the exception of one, all the respondents listed teachers first. Do teachers feel that they need the principal more than anyone else in the school? Do they think the principal's primary function is to assist *them*? Or is the order in which they identified the groups of no particular importance? I speculate about this only because the students, parents and community members interviewed for this book did not display the same self-focus when asked this question.

Teachers Need the Principal

Many of the ways teachers need the principal are described in the previous section, so I will not repeat them here. I will briefly describe any additional responses generated by this question.

Teachers need the principal to help them handle parent issues. They might need to mediate a parent–teacher conference or support a teacher's decision that is unpopular with a parent. One teacher seeks the principal's help when she has a "sticky parent situation." Only two teachers referred to needing the principal for help with student issues. One looks to the principal to "help make a decision about problem students." Another needs the principal to be "a go-to person for discipline issues." None of the teachers mentioned needing the principal's office as a place to send disruptive or troublesome students.

Some teachers need the principal to assist them with collegial relationships. A teacher asks, "Without a principal, what do I do about problems with relations between colleagues?" Another remarked, "We need someone to go to for personality conflicts—to act as a mediator." A third teacher admits, "Sometimes teachers can't work things out themselves." Teachers need to know there is someone at a higher level who can intervene when they have conflicts with their peers.

Many teachers look to the principal for recognition, validation, and accountability. Like anyone, teachers want to be recognized for a job well done, and the principal does this both formally (through evaluation instruments) and informally (through conversation and feedback). Teachers look to the principal for approval, to "validate what I'm thinking, how I handle a situation." Finally, some teachers recognize that the principal's authority holds them accountable. They need one "head person to see that things get done." The principal "creates a system of checks and balances" that ensures all the faculty and staff are fulfilling their responsibilities and no one "sloughs off."

Parents Need the Principal

The teachers interviewed for this book assume that parents need the principal for two reasons. First, they need someone to go to for problems. They mentioned problems with a teacher more often than problems with a student. Some just mentioned problems in general. Parents may need to ask questions, seek help, or make a complaint. Second, parents rely on the principal for communication—about the school and about their particular child.

Students Need the Principal

From the teacher perspective, students need a principal to help "keep them in line." The principal provides a higher level of authority—and a threat. "They need to know that someone can suspend them," explains one teacher. Another feels that "You're gonna go talk to the principal!" is an effective and needed discipline strategy. She also makes the point that this threat works only if the principal is a "revered person," someone the student respects and fears at the same time. Students need principals to provide structure, rules and expectations to help them manage their own behavior.

Teachers also believe that students need the principal "to talk to about problems" and "to look to as a role model." Students need to know that someone is watching over the school and making sure it runs smoothly. Only two teachers mentioned that students need the principal for educational reasons. As one explains, "The principal helps the teachers and it trickles down to them." Only one teacher identified "safe environment" as something students need principals to provide.

WHAT DO YOU THINK IT WOULD BE LIKE AT SCHOOL WITHOUT A PRINCIPAL?

Teachers agree with parents that it would be "chaotic" and "disorganized." No one would know what to do—or they just wouldn't do it. "A lot of little things wouldn't get taken care of." There would be no one to handle problems or hold people accountable.

Most teachers seem as fearful as students at the prospect of a school without a principal. Below are some of their reasons:

- Students would get out of control because there are no consequences.
- People would be quarreling and backstabbing. There would be a breakdown of relationships.
- It would be awful—no support system.
- There would be no way of making sure each teacher is doing his/her job.
- Some teachers would not be on top of things with nobody looking over their shoulders. Might not teach what they should.
- How will the teachers know what to do and when to do it? Who will I go to for help? Who's in the know?

Notice that these teachers are less concerned with the lack of student control as they are with the lack of teacher control. I was concerned that students and parents displayed little faith in the ability of teachers to govern themselves and the school in the absence of a principal. Now it appears teachers share this lack of confidence. What does this say about teachers? About the structure of schools? Is it themselves these teachers distrust or their peers?

Not all responses were entirely negative. One teacher who feels the school would be disorganized and disconnected also thinks it "might be more relaxed and creative." People might be willing to try new things. Another teacher feels that if a school "never had a principal," it might work. In other words, it might be possible to design a school to run successfully without a principal in charge. This same teacher felt that the sudden absence of a principal (here today, gone tomorrow!) would *not* work. "On a day-to-day basis in my classroom," explains a third teacher, "I don't think I'd see a lot of difference. But at a department level, a link would be missing for certain decisions."

> The most unique response to the question, "What would it be like at school without a principal?": "Who will run the meetings?"

IS THERE ANYTHING PRINCIPALS DON'T DO THAT YOU THINK THEY SHOULD?

Nearly a fourth of the teachers offered no suggestions. They either had no ideas or they felt the principal has enough to do already. One teacher thinks the principal should be a good curriculum leader. According to her, "I have worked with three principals. I never saw them work well with curriculum." All other responses to this question fell under one category.

The majority of teachers interviewed think principals should spend more time in classrooms. They provide a variety of reasons. Some are concerned about principals who have "been out of teaching for a long time." One explains, "If you've been a principal for twenty years you don' know what it's like anymore." Spending more time in classrooms will also help a principal get to know the students and the teachers better and "get a feel for what a typical day is like in the classroom." Teachers don't just want principals to come in for their annual evaluation visits, but to interact with the class and be "excited about what they're doing." One teacher thinks principals should still teach.

In the last chapter we found that parents think principals should be more visible and more involved with students and parents. Parents want to see the principal everywhere; teachers want to see the principal in the classroom. Of course there are always those teachers who would rather the principal *never* visit their classroom. Either I did not interview any of those teachers, or they didn't want to admit this thought to me. Generally speaking, though, I think principals can assume that teachers (and parents) do not want them to hide in the office and be disconnected from the classroom experience. They want principals to know what classroom life is like so they can provide better assistance and support to teachers, and have more influence on students.

> The most unique response to the question, "Is there anything principals don't do that you think they should?": "They should be forced to teach in some capacity."

WHAT DO YOU THINK WOULD BE HARDEST ABOUT THE JOB?

Teachers provided a variety of responses to this question, with only a few receiving multiple votes. As one might expect, discipline was cited most often (though not by a majority). In addition to having to deal with difficult students, teachers think it would be hard to deal with the parents of difficult students, specifically those "who think their kid doesn't do anything wrong." The second most frequent answer was "trying to please everybody." Teachers recognize that principals have to make decisions that are unpopular with some people. It would be hard to "develop a thick skin, to not take things personally." These top responses both focus on dealing with people.

Other shared responses focus on the management realm. A few teachers think the hardest part of the job would be juggling many responsibilities at the same time. It would be difficult to "maintain that focus and not get bogged down in the details." Several others referred to budget cuts, especially those that affect staff. "It would be hard deciding who gets cut." One teacher thinks the hardest part of the job would be dealing with administrative duties because she would "miss everyday interaction with students."

Other single responses include: *the political game playing that goes on, the time involved,* and *giving criticism to teachers who aren't doing well.* The fact that teachers have such diverse ideas about the most challenging aspects of the principalship suggests that teachers know a lot about the job. If teachers had a more limited view of the principal job, they would have fewer responsibilities to choose from and thus would offer more shared responses. This question also illustrates that from the teacher point of view almost everything principals do is difficult. Why would people choose this job? Let's see what teachers think.

WHY DO YOU THINK PEOPLE CHOOSE TO BECOME PRINCIPALS?

Considering the grim picture teachers painted of the principalship , it's no wonder the most popular responses to the question why do people choose to become principals pertain to self-advancement. To choose such a demanding job principals must see something in it for themselves. More than half of the teachers think people choose to become principals to escape the classroom. They are either "tired of teaching" or "don't like being in the classroom." One teacher surmises that "a couple stressful years in the classroom" could cause a teacher to look for another job, and the principalship is a logical next step. I know that some people become principals for this reason. One can only hope that it is not so prevalent a reason as these teachers suggest.

If teachers think a lot of principals are former burned-out teachers, why do they want them to spend more time in their classrooms? If most teachers (and other people as well) think many individuals choose the principalship to get out of the classroom, does that mean they think being a principal is an easier job? One teacher hinted at this when she said, "It's a way to be in the school setting without the stress of a classroom teacher." My face might have revealed my thoughts because she quickly added, "Well, you'd have different stress."

Many teachers also consider money to be a motivating factor for those who choose to become principals. Two even suggested that it is the number one reason. Similarly, teachers see the principalship as a way to "move up the ladder" and advance a career. One can't fault people for wanting to increase their salaries or improve their positions in the organizational hierarchy; in many businesses that's how success is defined. Yet, in the field of education most of us would rather see people choose a leadership position for more altruistic reasons. Fortunately, there are some.

Teachers do not think all principals are motivated by self-serving factors. A few perceive that some principals are born leaders and have a desire to improve education. They want the opportunity to "run a school the way they think it should be run." People may choose to become principals because they love children and have a strong desire to help others. And some "just like to be in charge." Most teachers agree that people aspire to the principalship for more than one reason, but their overall perceptions are decidedly cynical. That's not reassuring, considering today's teachers are tomorrow's potential principals.

> The most unique response to the question, "Why do you think people choose to become principals?": "I don't know because I wouldn't want to be one!"

SO, WOULD YOU WANT TO BE A PRINCIPAL?

Not one teacher said yes. A few said maybe; most said no. These teachers might consider money, career advancement and teacher burnout to be motivating factors for others, but they aren't for them. How about the opportunity to lead, to affect education on a larger scale? What about the students? The teachers I interviewed, both novice and veteran, see in the principalship more deterring factors than appealing ones.

These teachers perceive the principal role as one that involves too many problems, responsibilities, conflicts, and stress. They are not interested in the administrative aspects of being a principal: *supervising adults, being in the public eye, making the big decisions, dealing with the mundane tasks.* A few of the veteran teachers said they were once interested in the principal role but have since changed their minds. As one explains, "I've seen too many years of the reality of the job." I was originally pleased to see that the teachers I interviewed have such a knowledgeable perception of what principals do. Now I wonder if that isn't a detriment. It seems the more a person understands about the principal role, the less likely he or she wants to be one.

The three teachers who say they might consider being a principal are novice teachers with three or fewer years of experience. All three initially said they would *not* want to be a principal and then added, "maybe someday." As one would expect, these three teachers want to concentrate on teaching and gaining more experience before they consider moving to a leadership position. Even then, they have certain stipulations. For one the decision to become a principal "would depend on the school. Maybe in a small school where you could know everybody." This thought is echoed by another: "I wouldn't want to be a principal in a large school. I would want a close-knit family, and you can't do that in a large school like ours."

If other teachers in the field share the sentiments expressed above, what are the implications? The profession is experiencing a shortage of principals at the same time many districts are building bigger and bigger schools or consolidating small ones. Will the current teaching population produce enough principals to lead our schools tomorrow?

> The most unique response to the question, "So, would you want to be a principal?": "No. I don't want to be the person always being talked about."

WHO IS YOUR FAVORITE PRINCIPAL?

Though I prefaced this question with "Of all the principals you have known as a child or adult . . ." the majority of teachers chose a principal they have worked with professionally. Does that mean they didn't like the principals from their youth or they don't remember them? Or does it mean they are so immersed in their teaching roles that the principals they have known as adults are more notable? My guess is that the principal role is so important to teachers that their ideas of a favorite principal is one that has helped them the most in their career. Of course, some of them may not remember childhood principals—two of them told me so. The fact that most chose former or current employers is significant to me for one reason. It means their descriptions can help me learn what teachers value in a principal, and that knowledge might help me be a better one. I hope it might help others as well.

It is very important to these teachers that a principal be approachable and open-minded. One teacher's favorite principal created an atmosphere where "everyone felt welcome and comfortable going to see him." Another admired a principal who "was always willing to try new things." Good principals, from a teacher perspective, also welcome input and do not hold themselves "above" the teachers in an intimidating fashion. They are supportive and willing to help but aren't always "looking over your shoulder." Several teachers referred to the importance of displaying a balanced demeanor—friendly and open, but also firm and tough.

Teachers admire a principal who is organized and keeps them informed. Good principals also "push" their teachers and have high expectations for them. A principal who "forces teachers to think about what they are doing" is more admirable than the principal who allows teachers to be content with the status quo. Nobody described a favorite principal who kept to him/herself or allowed teachers to be completely autonomous. Most teachers want someone who provides direction and support while promoting improvement and innovation.

Teachers also admire principals who have good relationships with students. One teacher highlighted the importance of basing decisions "on if it is good for kids." Others are impressed with principals who spend a lot of time "connecting" with students, and who treat students with respect. One teacher was impressed with a principal simply because "he seemed to know each student in our school." None of the teachers described a principal who is strict and keeps the students in line. This doesn't mean teachers don't want principals to be strong disciplinarians; it is just not one of the qualities that makes a principal admirable. If "speak softly and carry a big stick" is your motto, you might find it more effective to "speak kindly and get rid of the stick."

> The most unique response to the question, "Who is your favorite principal?": "Definitely none from when I was a kid. I never knew those people."

WHAT DO YOU THINK PEOPLE LEARN ABOUT IN PRINCIPAL SCHOOL?

Fortunately, I did not have to explain principal school to any of the teachers. Nor were any of them surprised to find out principals are required to have more schooling. Two tried to get off easy by saying "I don't know," but I pushed them to consider, "What do you think you would need to learn about before becoming a principal?" Most could provide a list of possible topics. I list them below in order of frequency:

- Supervision and evaluation of personnel
- Budget and finance
- Management or administrative skills
- Interpersonal skills and human relations
- Discipline
- Legal issues
- Curriculum
- Building maintenance and operations
- Communication and home-school connection
- Public speaking
- Decision-making
- Educational trends and theory
- Resources—identifying and gathering
- Leadership
- How to run meetings
- Stress management
- Time management
- Psychology
- How to handle parents
- Goal setting
- Accreditation

What is there to learn from this list? Do teachers reveal any of their perceptions of the principal role? The order of the list has some significance. The first five items received more mentions than all the others combined. The last few items on the list were identified by only one or two teachers. What teachers think people learn in principal school illustrates their notions of what principals do. Principals supervise staff, work with a budget, handle administrative tasks, interact with people, and deal with discipline issues. Most teachers recognize those tasks as primary.

Very few of these teachers appreciate the extent to which principals need to understand school law, curriculum design, and leadership strategies. None of them identified the need for coursework in public relations, school-community relationships, philosophy or ethics. Is this significant? If teachers knew the myriad topics and skills addressed in principal training programs would it change their perceptions of the role? I'm not sure. With this particular group it might only increase their aversion to the principalship!

> The most unique response to the question, "What do you think people learn about in principal school?": "Do they have a Discipline 101?"

SOME CONCLUDING THOUGHTS ON WHAT TEACHERS THINK PRINCIPALS DO

I must admit that I expected to get more negative feedback from teachers about the principal position. Having spent many years as a teacher and being privy to the staff room gossip and hallway conversations, I know that teachers often see the principal as someone who doesn't understand their plight or requires them to do pointless things. As a principal, I have gained that uncanny knack mothers have of knowing what is going on behind my back. I have felt the collective eye roll when I turn to leave the faculty meeting. I have sensed the subtle opposition to tasks I ask teachers to do—the spoken or unspoken suggestion that this is just another hoop we have to jump through and has no connection to what we do in the classroom.

One of my favorite student quotes is the eighth grader's allegation that principals "go home and make lists of stuff they can do to kids to be mean." It's so absurd it makes me laugh every time I read it. Yet, I think it's highly probable that some teachers think principals go home and make lists of stuff they can do to teachers to be mean—or at least to be ridiculously irritating. Principals are administrators, and there's a perception in schools—and all hierarchical organizations—that the higher you go, the less you know. I remember joking to people when I was in "principal school" that when I finish this degree they'll suck half my brains out. There must be administrators that help to create this perception, which is then unfortunately applied across the board.

I am quite confident this perception of the principal role exists among the teaching population, but very little of it surfaced through the teacher interviews. Oh, I heard a rare comment now and then, like the teacher who doesn't want to be a principal because she "doesn't want to be the person always talked about." Or the two teachers who are critical of principals who have been out of teaching so long "they don't know what it's like anymore." For the most part, though, the teachers I interviewed were very nonjudgmental and often complimentary of principals. The reason is fairly obvious. I am a principal and these teachers know that. I'm not *their* principal, but I wear the hat. They likely held back some of their criticisms or negative assumptions out of pure kindness or tact.

There is one question, however, where the perception of principals as out-of-touch administrators is subtly indicated by most of the teachers. When asked what principals don't do but should, many said they should be in the classroom more. On the surface this may mean that teachers want principals to come into the classroom because it is good for students or their presence will somehow be helpful. I think it is more likely that teachers want principals to spend more time in the classroom because they don't have a clue about teaching and maybe spending time in classrooms will connect them to the real world. The statement that principals "should be forced to teach in some capacity" was probably completed in that teacher's head ". . . so they know what we have to go through."

I do have to give teachers credit for understanding a good deal about what principals do, however. They were able to identify many of the tasks and responsibilities. They seem to understand the scope and complexity of the role. Finally, they appreciate that the principalship is not easy and is often rife with conflict. At least they don't think principals sit in their office drinking free coffee all day. If they did, maybe more of them would have a desire to be principals. As it is, I'm a little worried about where the next generation of principals is going to come from.

Chapter Five

What Other Community Members Think Principals Do

INTRODUCTION

When I envisioned this book, I first wondered what students, parents, and teachers think about the principalship, because my everyday interactions with them suggested they might have misconceptions. But I was also interested in knowing what members of the greater community think. Numerous people not directly connected to schools have notions about how they operate. Their perceptions are rooted only in their pasts and thus may be different from those of people currently active in school life. Since it is becoming more and more important for schools to have community support and involvement, it would be helpful to understand how citizens in the community at large view schools and the people who lead them.

For this chapter I interviewed adults of all ages, from twenty-four to seventy-eight. They include both single and married people without children. I also included parents of grown children, most of whom are grandparents. The people in this group do not deal with schools on a day-to-day basis, but are able to reflect on their past student and parent experiences. This chapter will be shorter to avoid redundancy. In some ways the perceptions of these community members are similar to those of parents and even students. I will focus on where their perceptions appear to differ from those of the other groups.

WHAT IS A PRINCIPAL?

The definitions generated by community members are fairly typical and reflective of those discussed earlier. A principal is generally seen as *the head of the school, the person in charge,* and *an administrator.* Less common definitions include *leader, role model,* and *problem solver.* This question did not provide much in the way of revealing or unique perceptions.

WHAT DO PRINCIPALS DO?

Of all the groups interviewed, this one provided the widest *variety* of responses. They reiterated much of what I heard from others, but more of them provided longer lists and some of them brought up tasks heretofore unmentioned. Unlike the student and parent groups, I did not detect a lot of hesitancy or uncertainty as they answered. These people did not look to me for confirmation of their answers, nor did they guess or imagine. Only one of the community members said she had no idea what principals do, and she still managed to identify four responsibilities.

Students and parents made few references to the principal's role in teaching and learning—they focused on the disciplinary and managerial aspects. The community people also identified disciplinary and administrative tasks, but they balanced those with tasks focused on teaching and learning. Many of them described the principal's role in leading the teachers. They "have to see what the needs of teachers are," and "make sure the teachers are doing a great job." The adults in this group made many references to the development and supervision of curriculum and the provision of programs for students. Several explained that principals need to keep up with educational trends and help develop better teaching methods.

This group as a whole focused more on the educational responsibilities of principals than students or parents did. Why is that? All the people in the community group were once students and over half are parents of grown children. Wouldn't you expect their perceptions to mirror the other two groups since they are "former members?" I have a theory to explain the difference.

Although these community members are all former students, they are no longer children. As they reflect on their student experiences they now look through the eyes of adults. They focus less on the observable aspects of the principalship; they can see the bigger picture. These adults all know that the primary function of a school is to educate, thus the leader of the institution must be involved in the educational process. One might object that parents are also community members and adults. Why don't they share this perception? My theory extends to parents. When asked what principals do, parents understandably identify the things they see their child's principal doing on a daily basis. They don't *see* principals working with teachers to improve instruction. They don't *see* principals researching educational programs.

Community members, on the other hand, have the benefit of distance. Their descriptions of what principals do are based not on what they see principals do but on what they can reasonably assume would be part of the job. A further illustration of the distance factor is none of the community members mentioned that principals "wander the halls," as so many students and parents did. Only one of them said principals visit classrooms. Since these people aren't in schools, they don't observe the day-to-day activity of principals. They are more focused on the big picture.

> The most unique response to the question "What do principals do?": "When all else fails—discipline."

WHY DOES A SCHOOL NEED A PRINCIPAL?

When I asked this question of students, parents, and teachers, they tended to focus on how they in particular need the principal. The community group does not have this personal perspective. All of their responses to this question reflect a perception of the principal as the critical factor in school management. Some illustrative terms are: *centralized source of authority, backbone of the operation,* and *the steering wheel of the school.* The principal provides stability and direction, makes the decisions, and holds everyone else accountable. One middle-aged gentleman remarked, "No matter how good employees may be, they all require a boss." I find it interesting that the previous question revealed the community group's perception of the principal as an educational leader, while this question generated responses that focus on the school as a business and the principal as a manager.

> The most unique response to the question "Why does a school need a principal?": "To fix things."

WHO NEEDS THE PRINCIPAL?

The community members gave basically the same responses as the other groups. They identified most of the same reasons why students, parents and teachers need the principal. This question did not provide any additional insight into community members' perceptions of the principal role.

WHAT DO YOU THINK WOULD BE HARDEST ABOUT THE JOB?

This question generated quite a range of answers, most of which focus on human conflict: *conflicts between teachers, pleasing everybody, handling disagreements, everybody's got their complaints,* and *dealing with problem students* to name a few. There were very few references to the managerial aspects of the principalship. The perception these responses suggest is that principals must be people managers more than business managers. From this point of view, being a principal might be a fine job if there weren't any people in the school.

> The most unique response to the question "What do you think would be hardest about the job?": "Probably just showing up some days."

WHAT DO YOU THINK IT WOULD BE LIKE AT SCHOOL WITHOUT A PRINCIPAL?

The community members tied with the parents for the most instances of the word "chaos." It was by far the most frequent response to this question for both groups. Those who didn't use the term "chaos" disclosed similar sentiments with words like "dysfunctional," "unorganized," "bedlam," and "confusing." These adults also predicted that a school without a principal would be filled with "anxiety," "tension," and "poor morale."

Their perceptions do not paint a pretty picture, and, in fact, one person said "it would get ugly."

Very few members of this group felt student behavior would get out of hand, and only one was concerned that there would be "no one to put the teachers in line." It seems community members are more confident than the other groups that students and teachers could discipline themselves. Is this a more accurate perception of the way it would be, or are these community members looking through rose-colored glasses? Let's hope we don't ever have to find out.

> The most unique response to the question "What do you think it would be like at school without a principal?": "Somebody's going to get overwhelmed."

IS THERE ANYTHING PRINCIPALS DON'T DO THAT YOU THINK THEY SHOULD?

Nearly half of the community members could think of nothing. One confessed, "I'm stumped." The rest of them were most interested in seeing principals spend more time interacting with students. This is reflective of both the student and parent perspectives.

Several people think the principal should keep a tighter reign on their teaching staff. One wishes they would "give less control to teachers—keep an eye on them better." Another agrees that the principals should "observe teachers in the classroom more." And a third, "They should hold their staff accountable. I don't think they do that." These responses suggest more about the community's perception of teachers than of principals. I'm even more convinced someone should investigate the question: What do people think teachers do?

> The most unique response to the question, "Is there anything principals don't do that you think they should?": "Some of them could be better at their job."

WHY DO YOU THINK PEOPLE CHOOSE TO BECOME PRINCIPALS?

The members of this group provided all the answers identified by the others. The reason given most often was "they want to make a difference" or "to make schools better." Leadership tendencies and a love of children and education came in a close second. These responses correspond to the most frequent answers given by students and parents. Only two community members perceived the principalship as an escape from classroom teaching, and only one gave money as a motivating factor.

Now that we have the responses of all four groups, it's interesting to note that teachers are the only ones to identify teacher burnout and increased salary as the most likely reasons people choose to become principals. The other three groups cited altruistic reasons most often, with the community members exhibiting the most optimism. Why do those most removed from education hold principal motives in the highest regard? Is this simply wishful thinking? Or might they be less critical of principals because they don't deal with them on a daily basis? More significantly, what is the thought process of the teachers? Are they more cynical and pessimistic, or merely realistic? It is reasonable to assume teachers know best when it comes to this question. They interact with principals both professionally and socially; they are likely to have more insight into what attracts people to the job. Also, of all the people interviewed, only teachers are in a direct position to become principals themselves. Most have probably speculated about the principalship and in doing so considered the pros and cons of the job. I wonder if their perceptions reflect the true reasons people become principals?

One other interesting point surfaced with this question. People may become principals because they are encouraged or even persuaded by others to do so. A member of the community group suggested that some people become principals because "they were such good teachers everyone assumed they would be good principals." The suggestion is that this may not always be the case. Another person echoed this sentiment when he described his experience at the secondary level. "Many principals are former jocks, perhaps successful coaches. Because of that, people thought they would make good principals. Tough people, in other words!" The lesson to be learned from this is that success at one level does not guarantee success at another. If you are a principal looking to encourage others to consider this profession, ask not "Are they good at what they do" but "Will they be good at what *I* do?"

> The most unique response to the question, "Why do you think people choose to become principals?": "Some think they're going to change the system and all that happy stuff."

SO, WOULD YOU WANT TO BE A PRINCIPAL?

Community members might hold more noble perceptions of the rewards of the job, but they are no more likely than the others to be attracted to it themselves. Most community members would not want to be principals. It involves too much work and too much responsibility. They don't see themselves as suited for the job. "I don't have patience with children," and "I hate conflict," are typical explanations. One grandmother admitted, "I believe God created everyone for a job, and I wasn't created for that!" Another grandmother agrees, "I'm not cut out for that."

A few members of this group answered "yes" or "possibly" to the question. They are all men. That may surprise no one. The principalship is certainly a job that attracts more men than women. There are more men in principal positions, even at the elementary level where most classroom teachers are women. I don't know if it's significant that only men answered yes to this question in the community group, because I didn't find the same pattern in the other groups. I think the *reasons* they gave are significant. The men who might want to be principals provided the following explanations:

- Because I would get to boss people around. I think I could do it better than others.
- If I was in the educational system I probably would. I like to lead versus follow.
- All the administrative work is my cup of tea.
- If I'd chosen teaching as a profession I probably would have wanted to advance. Would want to have more say.

To be fair, one of these men did say he would like to have an influence in many students' futures, but he is also the one who said he would get to boss people around. These men are attracted to the principalship not because they like kids or want to improve education, but because no matter *what* field they are in they want to move up the level of command and have more control. Is this more typical of men than of women? Whether due to nature or nurture, I think there is some truth to that. Of the men I know who have become principals, most of them had that as an original career goal. When they entered teaching they did so with the intention of teaching for several years and then moving to the next level. For some the superintendency is their ultimate destination. On the other hand, a lot of the women principals I know (including myself) did not plan to be principals. They entered teaching because they loved kids, loved teaching or both. Somewhere along the way they either emerged as a leader in their schools or they developed a desire to have a broader impact on education (or they got tired of teaching). Maybe they were encouraged by others to consider the principalship. I'm not saying these scenarios are true of all men and women, but I think it may be a common pattern.

The most unique response to the question, "So, would you want to be a principal?": "No. I have no patience with children; I have no patience with parents of children."

WHO IS YOUR FAVORITE PRINCIPAL?

Sadly, several people in this group do not have a favorite principal. Not because they don't remember any, but because they don't remember any they liked. Age was not a factor here. A twenty-four year old man stated bluntly, "I can't remember any that I liked." A forty-three year old man admitted, "I never really cared for principals because I was a troublemaker and principals meant discipline to me." Even a seventy-year-old grandmother remembers that "I was scared to death of our first one. My high school principal? I can't say I *dis*liked him." Fortunately, not everyone has such a dismal history with principals.

Of the community members who identified a favorite principal, every one chose a principal from childhood. This surprised me. I expected that the older people (sixties and seventies) who had raised children would be more likely to choose one of their children's principals. First, because they would be easier to recall. Second, I tend to think that principals of long ago were more strict and intimidating than those of today. I believe my prediction has been the victim of stereotype. Their fondest principal memories took these adults back to their elementary and high school days, which adds a perception we have not yet seen. Parents of school-age children reflected mostly on principals in their children's schools, and the teachers chose principals for whom they had worked. This is our first peek at how childhood impressions of principals stand the test of time. For what are they likely to be remembered?

The favorite principals this group described shared many common characteristics. They were nice people who cared about kids and treated them with respect. They "talked to everyone," and made them feel "comfortable" and "important." A few referred to their favorite principal as being strict. One retired doctor reminisced about his high school principal, "He instilled the fear of God in you." Though they were strict, these principals were also "fair," "kind," and "humane." Many used the positive, though generic term "nice" to describe the one principal they remember most positively.

Other than one reference to a principal who was organized, none of these people described the administrative competencies of their favorite principals. We don't know if they made good management decisions or supervised staff effectively. Were they educational leaders or diligent managers? Did they know how to manage a budget, implement curriculum, and oversee the day-to-day operations of a school?

These are some of the many qualifications and skills required of an effective principal, and perhaps many of the favorite principals described above possessed some of these capacities. However, when people look back over time, what they remember most and what *matters* most is the type of *person* a principal was. This reminds me of a question I once encountered in a job interview: What do you want people to say about you at your retirement party? In other words, what do you want to be remembered for? I don't think principals should try to win popularity contests or be consumed with people liking them all the time (the fact is, everybody won't), but it is important to consider the impact of our actions and words. Education is a people industry, not a product industry. If we focus only on the tasks and the problems and neglect human relationships, we have done only part of what we are called to do. I am grateful to these nostalgic citizens for reminding me of that.

The most unique response to the question, "Who is your favorite principal?: "Never met him."

WHAT DO YOU THINK PEOPLE LEARN ABOUT IN PRINCIPAL SCHOOL?

Once again I received a few incredulous replies. "There's a principal school?" One person just assumed I was being hypothetical and stated knowingly, "If there *was* a principal school people would learn. . . ." As with the parents, I explained to these skeptics about principal training and licensure, and again some were surprised to find out such requirements exist. There must be others beyond the education profession who are ignorant of the additional educational training required of principals, and it must have some impact on their perceptions of the job. I don't know how much confidence and trust I would have in my accountant, airline pilots or the family vet if I didn't know they needed specialized training for their jobs.

For those who did know about principal training, or conceded that point, the most often repeated topics were management skills and financial issues. Principals should be taught how to "organize things," "plan or deal with a budget" and "raise funds." Some less frequent replies include "psychology," "leadership skills," "staff management," and "handling students." A host of other ideas received mention by only one or two people: *test scores, PR skills, curriculum, building maintenance,* and *educational philosophy.*

This group also suggested some ideas of what people *should* learn in principal school. These ideas focus on social skills and "getting along with people." Principals should learn how to "gain people's trust," " be a good listener," and "have compassion." We might even "learn to have charisma." These responses correspond to this group's memories of principals who were nice, kind and respectful.

The community members I interviewed have suggested in several ways that principals should be good people, not just good managers. People look to them as role models. They are remembered for their interpersonal skills. Do principal training programs include this emphasis? I am sure it depends on the program and the school. I would venture to guess that most principal training programs touch on the development of ethical, just, and caring leaders, but such concepts likely take a back seat to school law, budget and finance, supervision, and curriculum management. Principal training programs are designed to meet state licensure requirements and national standards for school administrators. Thus, their focus tends to be on the business side of schooling more than the human side. If university training programs do not emphasize the human dimensions of leadership, aspiring principals (and those already in the field) may want to consider developing these characteristics through other means—unless, of course, they come to you naturally!

> The most unique response to the question, "What do you think people learn about in principal school?": "How to handle crabby parents."

SOME CONCLUDING THOUGHTS ON WHAT COMMUNITY MEMBERS THINK PRINCIPALS DO

Responses from community members proved to be surprising. I expected their perceptions of the principal role to be fairly limited and mostly negative. Since they don't deal directly with schools, their perceptions are based on the past and on what they read in the newspaper about schools. From the older community members, especially, I expected to hear frightening recollections of cruel disciplinarians and grueling taskmasters. I was pleased to find many of them understand that principals have many responsibilities, not the least of which are related to teaching and learning. It was also heartening to learn that many ordinary citizens have positive recollections of principals, even the strict ones.

What I learned most from this group is that the distance of both place and time has an impact on one's perception of what principals do. Students, parents, and teachers are often too close to the principal role to see the bigger picture. They are very focused on what they *see* principals do, what they *know* principals do, and what they *need* principals to do. Community members, on the other hand, are more likely to draw assumptions about the less obvious roles that principals fill. They are also more optimistic about the motivations of people who become principals. I began this book expecting the community group's perceptions to be either disheartening or deficient; for the most part they turned out to be quite the opposite.

Chapter Six

How Hollywood Portrays Principals

INTRODUCTION

When I began outlining this book, I was first interested in how different people think about the role of the principal, and then I began to consider how those perceptions are formed. I believe most perceptions of the principal role are a result of one's direct experience with principals—as a student, a teacher, or a parent. But I also investigated the extent to which those perceptions might be shaped by the way the entertainment media portrays principals.

Early in my teaching career, I became aware of how teachers were portrayed in movies and on television. It seemed like they were always boring drones, bumbling imbeciles, or cruel taskmasters. When I became a principal I noticed the same thing about the media's depiction of principals. It troubled me to think that both children and adults might consider principals in movies to be typical of real principals. I wondered if that is how we really appear to the people with whom and for whom we work.

Although I had my own theory about principals in film, I knew I must test that theory. My general determination, before I started my research, was that principals are almost always portrayed negatively, which might cause people—both children and adults—to think of principals in a negative light. Of course, I realized that my theory might be skewed by the limited number of movies to which I had been exposed. I decided to watch as many movies as I could to help answer the following questions: 1) Are principals painted in a negative way by those who seek to entertain us? and 2) If yes, what implications does this hold for principals and the people they serve?

A PARADE OF PRINCIPALS

I had a difficult time coming up with a lengthy list of movies involving principals, so I decided to go to the "experts." First I asked some high school students, and they pointed me toward titles I had never heard of. Then I went to my neighborhood video rental store and told the (young) employees about my book and asked for their assistance in developing a list of movies with school settings and particularly with principals in either major or minor roles. They were more than happy to oblige and sent me away that first night with five movies and the promise to work on a list. By the next day I had a list of over twenty movies.

Then I began my "research," which consisted of spending entire evenings and weekends watching movies. Many movies with principals as characters are written for children or teenagers, and these movies are set in *their* world, the world of school. So I found myself watching hour after hour of what some call "teeny-bopper flicks." By the end of the third day, I began to worry whether I would ever again be able to put several words together to form a coherent sentence—and one not involving profanity. I believe I survived with my brain intact, but I'll leave it up to the reader for the final evaluation. I have to admit that I received some comic satisfaction from telling friends I was busy this weekend doing "research for my book."

I considered many ways of summarizing what I learned from my "couch research," and decided to deal with each movie individually. Sometimes, paraphrased material loses a lot in the translation. Therefore, to support my arguments, I include a fair number of direct quotes from the movies I watched.

I began with a movie that does not necessarily target a young audience; the material and the message are of an adult nature, as the film's perspective is through the eyes of a teacher, not a student. The movie is *Dangerous Minds*, with Michelle Pfeiffer in the lead role. This movie is about an ex-Marine in the process of earning her teaching credentials. She interviews for what she thinks is a student teaching assignment and walks out of the school with a long-term substitute position. She is excited at the prospect, until she spends a few moments in her class. The movie takes place in an inner city school where the kids are rough, disrespectful of adults, and facing issues related to poverty, drugs, violence, and a society in which they do not feel they have a place.

The principal in *Dangerous Minds* is a man devoted to rules and order—to a fault. When the new teacher comes to his office to tell him of something she feels is important, his first response is, "Miss Johnson, this is an office. We knock before we enter." Later in the movie a student comes to the principal to tell him he (the student) has been threatened by another student. The principal tells the student's teacher, Miss Johnson, "I sent him away—because he didn't knock. I'm trying to teach these kids to live in the world, and in the world you don't just burst into a person's office." The student is killed that day. As a viewer, one is overcome with the irony that a man who is "trying to teach these kids to live in the world" sends a student off to be killed because he didn't knock on the door.

This same principal is also highly fearful of lawsuits and would rather follow the book than do what's best for students or teachers. When Miss Johnson spends her first class period teaching kids karate moves—as a way of connecting with them and earning their respect—she is reprimanded by the principal, because "teaching karate is against school policy and can lead to a lawsuit." His words of wisdom to this beginning teacher are: "You're going to have to go along with our policies even if you don't agree with them." Certainly school policies are important, and teachers should abide by them, but might it not be more helpful to first recognize the teacher's good intentions and then offer some advice on more appropriate methods? The principal depicted in *Dangerous Minds* does not appear interested in the education of students or the professional development of teachers; his agenda consists of maintaining a position of power while covering his own backside.

In my judgment, the principal in *Dangerous Minds* plays the role of an antagonist in the film. It was very clear that if Miss Johnson is going to make a difference with students, it will be in *spite* of the principal, not because of him. Throughout the film he is portrayed as aloof, out of touch with the world of his students, and of little or no use to the teachers. His expectations for students are low, and he does not exhibit any redeeming qualities like kindness, compassion or a desire to help. As you watch this movie, you wonder why teachers would continue to work under such "leadership"—especially for the $24,000 a year Miss Johnson is offered as a first-year teacher. My first "research subject" went a long way toward confirming my theory that principals are portrayed very negatively in film.

In *The Substitute*, you can view another inner-city high school through the eyes of Hollywood. The principal in this film is a former policeman who rules his Miami high school in expensive suits. His large and lavishly furnished office looks out of place in a dilapidated, poorly equipped school. Like the principal in *Dangerous Minds*, this one also reveals his leadership style through his advice to a teacher: "Power perceived is power achieved. I'd remember that little truism, Mr. Smith. It will assist you greatly in your teaching."

Early in the movie we learn where this principal's priorities lie. He refuses to expel a student who threatens a teacher because he fears a lawsuit. Or so he says. We soon learn that he has even worse reasons for taking the student's side against the teacher's: he's a crook.

The polished, well-mannered principal turns out to be a drug dealer and a murderer, and to make matters worse, he funnels the drugs and money through the school. He is in league with gang members within the school and drug dealers on the outside. When the substitute teacher begins to suspect the illegal activity, the principal orders his student henchmen to kill the substitute. In the end, good does triumph over evil; unfortunately the evil to be expunged is the principal.

In *187* the story begins in New York at yet another inner city school rife with vandalism, violence, and poor leadership. The main character, a teacher, is threatened by a student. Mr. Garfield goes to the principal with a textbook in which this student has scrawled the number "187" on every page—which we learn is the police numerical reference for a homicide. The teacher takes this to mean that his life is being threatened and understandably seeks help from the principal.

The principal's response upon looking at the vandalized book is, "Does he [the student] know we have a budget problem?" His first concern is with the cost of replacing the textbook. When Mr. Garfield explains the significance of the message, the principal replies with an obvious lack of concern, "If I had a dollar for every student who threatened a faculty member. . . ." He further demonstrates his lack of human compassion when he tells Mr. Garfield, "You know what your problem is? On the one hand, you think someone is trying to kill you, and on the other you actually believe kids pay attention in your class." So much for emotional and professional support.

As one might expect, the student threat is real; Mr. Garfield is attacked in the hallway by the student and stabbed numerous times with an ice pick. As in *The Substitute*, the viewer is likely to conclude that the principal's lack of leadership leads to a violent act in the school. In this case the victim does not die. We catch up with Mr. Garfield eighteen months later in Los Angeles when he returns to the profession as a substitute teacher.

Mr. Garfield takes a long-term substitute position in an overcrowded school where his classroom is one of a string of trailers. He meets one of his new colleagues in the staff room and receives the following advice: "Don't look to the administration for support. They haven't been in the classroom in the last ten years. They don't know shit." And a little later, "Have you met Garcia yet—our principal?" The unspoken suggestion is that if you haven't, you aren't missing much.

A second colleague tells Mr. Garfield of a recent situation involving a student and her attempt to seek help from the principal. "This kid is threatening me," she relates, "and all Garcia cares about is a lawsuit." Hey! Which movie am I watching? I think I've seen this principal somewhere before.

Finally, Mr. Garfield meets the infamous Garcia when he is called to the office. He is instantly put on guard when he finds the teacher union representative also in attendance, and Garcia tells him that the conversation will be taped. The meeting is to address Mr. Garfield's accusation that a student stole his heirloom watch during a class experiment. Garcia informs Mr. Garfield that he thinks of students as his clients and it's his job to protect them (not a bad philosophy, maybe this guy isn't so bad). The suggestion is made that Mr. Garfield's accusation of theft is a slanderous statement that could lead to a lawsuit by the student. "We can't have another lawsuit," Garcia warns Mr. Garfield. "The last one cost the district a quarter million dollars." Ah, so it's not *really* the students he's trying to protect. Garcia is just another example of school administration concerned with covering its own backside.

Another point against Garcia (in my opinion) is the eventual discovery that he was never a teacher. "Teaching and being a principal don't necessarily go hand-in-hand, Mr. Garfield," he pronounces. The interview research I conducted for this book would suggest quite the opposite.

The rest of this movie focuses entirely on Mr. Garfield and his unfortunate moral and physical demise. We see no more of Garcia, but I believe his leadership style has been clearly defined and tends to support my theory that Hollywood does little to promote admiration for school principals.

It was time for some lighter fare. From the serious movies described above, with their dark and dismal reflections on American schools, I turned toward the humorous genre. This also appeared to be a move out of the inner city to the suburbs where principals aren't so much cruel as they are fools. Here began my foray into the world of "teeny-bopper flicks."

Ferris Bueller's Day Off is heralded by many people I know as the funniest movie they have ever seen. Though I can appreciate the humor appeal this movie has for young people in particular, I watched it with a critical eye on the principal role, which left me shaking my head in dismay more often than it left me slapping my knee in merriment.

To be accurate, there is no *principal* in *Ferris Bueller's Day Off*, but rather a dean of students. The role is the same, however. In larger high schools the assistant principal or dean of students is the one charged with handling student issues. In this case the dean, Mr. Rooney, considers himself charged with the sole task of "getting" Ferris Bueller—of finally beating him at his own game.

Ferris is a likable high school senior who is dedicated to having fun, usually at the expense of his education. He has perfected the art of faking illness in order to be excused from school. This movie chronicles the events of one such day in the life of Ferris Bueller. While his parents think he is home in bed, Ferris gallivants all over Chicago with his girlfriend and his best friend.

Mr. Rooney, the dean of students, is on to Ferris. When Ferris's mother calls him in sick, Mr. Rooney is quite certain that Ferris is up to his usual game of skipping school, and he smiles at the prospect of catching Ferris and keeping him from graduating. He becomes quite giddy as he plans how he will trap Ferris in his own game. "I'm gonna catch this kid and I'm gonna put one hell of a dent in his future. Fifteen years from now when he looks back on the ruin his life has become, he's gonna remember Edward Rooney."

It isn't bad enough that Mr. Rooney is more concerned with ruining a student than with educating him; he also displays unprofessional and immature behavior to his secretary. He barks orders at her and demeans her with phrases like, "Go soak your head," and "You pinhead." Throughout the movie he gives vent to a host of profanity and vulgar language.

But it isn't Mr. Rooney's meanness or unprofessionalsim on which this movie focuses. It is his stupidity. As his secretary tells him, "[Ferris] makes ya look like an ass is what he does, Ed." Throughout the movie, that is *exactly* what Mr. Rooney looks like. He leaves the school in search of Ferris and bumbles from one embarrassing situation to another. While trying to peek in the Buellers' windows he falls down, gets his shoes stuck to the ankle in oozing mud, and accidentally turns on the hose, which soaks him from head to toe. He peeks through the doggy door and comes face-to-face with the drooling, snapping family pet that proceeds to chase him around the yard and eventually traps him behind the fence. A bedraggled Mr. Rooney looks on while the dog chews his shoe. Meanwhile his car is towed for illegal parking.

By the end of the movie Mr. Rooney is reduced to a battered, bruised, mumbling idiot limping down the sidewalk. His pants are split in the seat and his shoes hang in tatters from his feet. A school bus rolls by and stops. The driver asks Mr. Rooney if he wants a ride. Mr. Rooney climbs on and is greeted by gaping-mouthed children who are probably wondering, "What happened to *him*?" He settles next to a particularly nerdy girl who offers him some candy she's been keeping in her pocket all day so it's nice and warm. Meanwhile, back at the Bueller home, Ferris makes it safely back to bed a split second before his parents return from work. He is greeted with loving concern and the promise of some warm soup. Ferris Bueller—the rule-breaking, dishonest, irresponsible student—is the winner. He triumphs at the expense of incompetent authority. And everybody cheers.

The Breakfast Club is another movie aimed primarily at a teenage audience. Though it differs from *Ferris Bueller's Day Off* in its inclusion of some serious, thought-provoking character development, it casts a similarly insipid and incompetent man in the role of principal. Like *Ferris Bueller*, this movie also tells the story of just one eventful day in the life of high school students.

The five main characters are high school students who have been assigned to a full day of detention for various offenses. They congregate in the school library on a Saturday morning and are greeted by their principal, Richard Vernon. Mr. Vernon lays out the day's agenda in an authoritative tone. "Ponder the error of your ways. You will not talk. You will not move from your seats. *We* are going to write an essay of no less than a thousand words on who you think you are." His use of "we" is reminiscent of the condescending nurse who asks, "How are *we* feeling today?"

Through his words and actions, Mr. Vernon presents a tough-guy, I'll-straighten-you-out attitude. He warns one student, "Don't mess with the bull, young man. You'll get the horns." Other examples: "Want me to yank you out of that seat?" "The next time I have to come in here, I'm crackin' heads!" In his attempts to gain control of the students, Mr. Vernon resorts to threats he can't keep. Although he plays tough, he really has very little authority with the kids. It is obvious they consider him a joke. This is exemplified in one scene where Mr. Vernon yells at the group, "I will not be made a fool of!" and then storms out of the library with a paper toilet-seat protector hanging from the waistband of his pants. He later finds one student alone, the one student he believes to be the leader of the rebellious clan. He calls the student a punk and admonishes, "That's the last time you ever make me look bad in front of these kids!" Of course, it isn't.

Like *Ferris Bueller's* Mr. Rooney, Mr. Vernon appears to be caught up in the power of his role—mainly the power to control, demean, and punish students. He sees his relationship with students as primarily adversarial. There is the slightest suggestion, however, that this was not always the case. In one scene he shares a beer with the custodian in a basement storage room and reflects on his career. The viewer is led to believe that Mr. Vernon once enjoyed his work, but somewhere along the way things changed. "These kids turned on me," he laments. "They think I'm a big f***ing joke." He also shares his fear that "when I get older these kids are gonna take care of me." (The custodian tells him not to count on it.)

In this movie we are given a brief glimpse at the human side of the principal, but for the most part he is portrayed as a bitter, vengeful disciplinarian and a bumbling fool. Once again, a significant part of the story's plot is the student-principal conflict, and the viewer is inclined to root for the students.

I'm going to dedicate very little space to the movie *Election* because its portrayal of the principal takes a back seat to a host of other issues that gave rise to both my eyebrows and my heart rate—among them, teacher indiscretion with a student, rampant profanity, fairly risqué sex scenes, marital infidelity, and glorified dishonesty. But I digress.

For the first half of *Election* my research notebook reflected only the following banal notes about the principal role: "not bad; kind of blah;

stereotypical male principal who uses trite phrases." Later in the movie I downgraded him to "unprofessional" when he says of a student: "That little bitch made a fool out of us. I want her out of the election! She's a troublemaker; she's on my list." Then he suspends the girl for three days on bogus grounds. He reaches "*highly* unprofessional" status when he demands of a teacher, "Where the hell have you been?"—in front of the students. Then I quit watching.

You may be wondering, are they really *all* bad? I wondered the same thing at one point in my research. I'm happy to report that the answer is no. I found one movie where the principal was only half-bad. *Light It Up* is a movie about a high school student who takes a security guard and several students hostage in protest of the deplorable condition of the school (overcrowding, leaking roof, no heat). This situation is precipitated by the suspension of a teacher that the students like.

A broken window and no heat send a teacher and his class in search of a more comfortable place to hold class. When they find the lunchroom, the library, and every spare room occupied with similarly displaced classes, the teacher leads his class to the principal's office. He is told, "Take them anywhere," and so the teacher does—to a nearby diner. Unfortunately, while they are there, the diner is held up by an armed assailant.

The teacher, our hero, disarms the assailant before anyone is hurt, but he is reprimanded for endangering the lives of his students by taking them off campus. The principal yells, "This is my pension, man! I got no choice; you're suspended." When a student reminds the principal that he said, "Take them anywhere," he responds with, "This does not concern you. Go back to your class." The students begin chanting in protest, security is called, a guard is injured, and the hostage situation ensues.

So what makes this man half bad (and thus, half good)? First of all, you can't blame him for reprimanding the teacher who takes students off campus. This is obviously a situation that puts both student safety and school liability at risk. Concern with student safety is a good thing. On the other hand, he makes a comment about his pension, which suggests he is more concerned with his own welfare than with his students'. That's a bad thing. Also, he does not accept any responsibility for the conditions that led to the teacher's actions. He offered no solution to the problem except to say, "Take them anywhere," and when reminded of his words he overreacts. That's another bad thing. Then, later in the movie he exhibits some concern for the school and the students during the hostage ordeal. He asserts (I think it was to the television reporter) that "most of the kids in my school are fine young men and women." That's a good thing. But, maybe he just said that to look good on television. *Light It Up* was a little less cut and dried than the movies previously discussed. I didn't necessarily applaud the principal, but I also didn't find him to be cast in an exclusively negative light. There is hope for the movie principal.

I was surprised to find a movie simply titled, *The Principal*. I was even more surprised to find that the title character is better than half bad; in fact, I'd call him mostly good. I say *mostly* good because he doesn't start out that way, and even after his transformation there are a few rough edges.

The Principal begins in a bar where Rick Latimer (our principal to be) throws back shots with his friends. He sees his ex-wife across the room with another man, the same man who served as her attorney during the divorce. Motivated by jealous rage and too much alcohol, Rick grabs a baseball bat from behind the bar and goes after his wife's companion. They end up in the parking lot where Rick uses the bat to ruin the other man's Porsche while the frightened attorney cowers inside it. Rick ends up at the police station where an officer asks, "Occupation?" Rick replies, "School teacher." It is not a response the viewer is expecting.

Next we see Mr. Latimer in his classroom where he uses binoculars to watch kids as they work. We follow his gaze to some shapely legs under a desk, then the bell rings and class dismisses. As the students file past his desk, Mr. Latimer says aloud, "Linda, I want you wearing a bra to class— or I'm gonna change your grade." So far our main character has given us little to admire. When he is called to a meeting of the school board, the viewer likely expects a reprimand—as does Mr. Latimer. No one is more surprised than he when the board offers him a principal position.

We soon find out that this is not so much a promotion as it is a punishment. Brandel High is a dilapidated school in the "bad" part of town. Like so many of the schools depicted in film, this school suffers the effects of poverty, violence, and drugs. The teachers are burned out and apathetic. The head of security informs Mr. Latimer that "most of the students here have been expelled from someplace else—permanently." A particularly nasty gang leader has the school in the grip of fear. Mr. Latimer hasn't moved *up* the ladder; he's moved down.

Mr. Latimer rises to the challenge, however. He takes a look at the many offensive things going on in "his school" and decides to put a stop to them. He calls a student assembly (against the fearful protests of teachers) and delivers a "no more" speech—no more drugs, no more skipping, no more violence. Of course, his message is not well received by the student body. A fight breaks out and Mr. Latimer's first attempt at order deteriorates before his eyes.

He perseveres. Mr. Latimer beefs up security and charges them with cleaning up the halls and making sure students go to class. When the teachers complain about now having to deal with the thugs in class, Mr. Latimer gives them a heartfelt, inspiring speech:

> You can't pick and choose your students. You gotta take the students the school gives you and teach them the best you can. You can't just teach the easy ones.

He implores the teachers to have courage in the face of challenges. Mr. Latimer models this courage as he faces one challenge after another, including a severe beating by the ruling gang.

Mr. Latimer also displays a commitment to the education of his students. He goes to school at 6:00 in the morning in order to tutor a girl who is ready to drop out. He finds time in his busy day to meet with a boy who has never learned to read, and he teaches him how. He inspires the teachers and gives hope to the students. In Mr. Latimer we see the ugly duckling become almost a swan. As I said before, he still has a few rough edges—like smoking in the school building and using profanity with both teachers and students. Considering the setting he is in, and the school he is charged with leading, the viewer can easily overlook such indiscretions. Finally, I found a movie principal with more good attributes than bad.

My search then took me back in time to a classic movie about school, *To Sir, With Love*. This movie from the 1960s is about an inspiring teacher, played by Sidney Poitier, who takes a group of rough students in a tough London school and turns them into young ladies and gentlemen. On his first day, he is labeled by a colleague as "the new lamb for the slaughter." My first observation upon viewing this movie is that times sure have changed. What this movie considers aberrant student behavior (throwing spitballs, knocking books off the desk, smoking) is mighty tame next to that found in movies today. But we must evaluate the movie within the context of its time.

If you have seen *To Sir, With Love*, you probably have a strong recollection of Poitier's character, Mr. Thackery. You may not recall much, if anything, about the role of the principal. Let me describe him for you. He is an older man, soft spoken and pleasant. He welcomes Mr. Thackery to the school by asking him why he wants to teach. Then he informs Mr. Thackery that "most of our children are rejects from other schools." He doesn't appear to be making a negative judgment of the students, simply stating a fact. He provides the following advice:

> We have to help them as best we can. We have to teach them *what* we can and *as much* as we can. The local authorities are not totally on our side. Of course, I and the staff will do everything we can to help you, but your success or failure will depend entirely upon you.

Although the principal puts a lot on Mr. Thackery's shoulders, he appears to be a caring man, willing to help. He is simply painting a realistic picture.

Mr. Thackery begins to make some progress with his students, and they ask him to take them on a field trip to a museum. He seeks approval from the principal, who is rather skeptical. He cautions Mr. Thackery about the likelihood that "it won't work," and he won't be able to control his class. The principal is willing to keep an open mind, however, and tells Mr. Thackery that if he can get another teacher to go along on the trip, then it will be approved. He keeps his word and the trip takes place.

For the most part, this principal comes across in a fairly positively light. He isn't a hero or even an inspirational leader. He is simply a pleasant man trying to do the best he can. He exhibits no inappropriate behaviors or major deficiencies. On a scale of one to ten, I'd give this principal a six.

Like dessert, I have saved the best high school movie for last. *Music of the Heart* tells the inspiring story of one woman's quest to share her love of music with children in New York's inner city schools. She is supported in her work by a strong and compassionate female principal.

The main character is a recently divorced mother of two who suddenly finds herself in need of an income. An accomplished violinist who has taught her two sons to play, she offers her skills as a violin teacher at a neighborhood school. Though skeptical at first, the principal is open-minded enough to consider the offer because it would be good for her students. She even stands firm against the school's music director, who opposes the idea because he doesn't think their students are capable of learning the violin. The principal has faith in both the students and the teacher and offers her a temporary position as violin instructor.

Later in the movie, the principal exhibits other positive attributes. Her actions and words suggest she truly cares about her students. She holds them to high standards of behavior without use of threats or power. This principal is also committed to solving problems, not avoiding or aggravating them. In one scene, we see her in the role of a skilled and caring mediator. She handles a conflict between a parent and the violin teacher saying, "I don't think we have an impossible situation here." She makes a suggestion to which both the parent and teacher agree. She displays the respect and compassion lacking in the other movie principals I viewed.

The principal is not a mealy-mouthed, pushover, however. She speaks her mind and isn't afraid to be painfully candid when she feels the situation warrants it. For example, when the violin teacher's own son gets into some trouble at school, the principal blatantly tells her, "Nick is in trouble and you need to deal with it." Her words compel the mother to recognize that her son's behavior is too serious to ignore.

The principal becomes a huge supporter of the flourishing violin program. She leads a standing ovation at the first concert and appears to be sincerely moved by the students' joy and success. She shows her strongest support when, after ten years, the program is in danger of cancellation due to district budget cuts. When her pleas to the school board fall on deaf ears, the principal joins a group of parents and teachers in a fight to save the program. She meets with them in their homes, and together they develop a plan to raise enough funds to save the program.

This principal epitomizes what most people look for in school leadership—commitment, energy, honesty, resiliency, and a true love and concern for children. It is interesting to note that this film is based on a true story. In the sampling of movie principals I selected, one might conclude that truth is better than fiction.

With the exception of that one heart-warming, inspiring movie, it is my conclusion that Hollywood's portrayal of high school principals appears decidedly negative. Maybe elementary principals are given a better break.

Or maybe not. Of the six elementary principals I viewed in film, not one of them left me feeling warm and fuzzy about the role.

The title character in *Matilda* is a seven-year-old girl who attends a rather frightening elementary school. If you could look up "worst principal ever" in the dictionary you would likely see a picture of Miss Trunchbill. Miss Trunchbill is every child's nightmare. She is a large, severely dressed woman who regularly snaps a riding crop to punctuate her verbal threats. She looks like the stereotypical prison guard, and to complete the picture she treats children more like hardened inmates than like students. Miss Trunchbill's motto is: "Use the rod, beat the child!" She employs both physical and psychological abuse to keep students in line with her rules. In her office she throws darts at a board covered with student photos. And then there's the chokey. Watch the film if you want to see Miss Trunchbill's unique and probably effective behavior management tool.

I enjoyed watching this movie for the pure and simple reason that it completely supported my theory about principals in film. Everything Miss Trunchbill did or said screamed of cruelty. To illustrate, I share some of her choicest quotes below:

> They're all mistakes, children. Filthy, nasty things. Glad I was never one of 'em.'
>
> You're mommy is a twit. (Swings the girl by pigtails and throws her over the fence)
>
> My idea of a perfect school is one in which there are no children.
>
> In this classroom, in this school, I am God!

Miss Trunchbill does do one thing that all good principals should do—she visits classrooms on a regular basis. The difference is that when a teacher knows Miss Trunchbill is scheduled to visit, she directs her students to prepare the room by removing every vestige of color and cheerfulness. The room is stripped of anything interesting. Attractive bulletin boards are replaced by a dull blackboard and a plain sign that reads, *If you are having fun, you are not learning.*

I'm sure you get the picture. Miss Trunchbill emulates every characteristic we do not want to see in a principal—or in any person for that matter. Not only did Miss Trunchbill dispel my hope that elementary principals might receive better depiction in film than high school principals, she also put to rest my growing suspicion that negative movie principals were limited to those of the male persuasion. Further viewing verified that negative portrayal of principals is an equal opportunity art form.

Uncle Buck is a movie that has more to say about the parent role than it does about the principal role, but it offers one scene that furthers my theory about Hollywood principals. Enter another severely attired, female principal who has managed to choose a career that involves children despite her obvious abhorrence for them.

Uncle Buck is left with the temporary task of caring for his two nieces and one nephew when their parents are called out of town for a family emergency. A conference with the principal, scheduled before his appearance on the scene, falls on Uncle Buck's shoulders. He enters the principal's office, becomes transfixed with the oversized, unsightly mole on her chin, and is instantly transformed into a babbling, stuttering fool. He is catapulted back to his senses when the principal opens her mouth and spews forth the following evaluation:

> I've been an educator for thirty-one point three years and in that time I've seen a lot of bad eggs. I say eggs because at the elementary level we are not dealing with fully developed individuals.

And she continues:

> I see a bad egg in your niece. She's a twiddler, a dreamer, a silly-heart, a jabber-box, and I don't think she takes a thing in her life or her career as a student seriously.

The child she is talking about is six years old! Uncle Buck puts this principal in her place, telling her that he would be sad if a six-year old girl was *not* a silly-heart and a dreamer. He makes some nasty threat about the principal ever messing with his niece and leaves her with her mouth gaping open. That is the one and only time we see this principal, but it is enough. She, too, exemplifies the Hollywood stereotype that principals are either incompetent fools, malicious child-haters, or both.

Snow Day begins with the narration, "Meet Principal Ken Weaver, a man who was number one on every kid's winter hit parade." We see Mr. Weaver in his back yard, dressed in "geeky" clothing, tending to his barbecue grill. Children on a nearby roof pelt him with manufactured snowballs from a cooler (it has yet to snow in this small town, despite the date on the calendar). It's obvious how children feel about Mr. Weaver; I wonder how he feels about them? We soon find out.

Mr. Weaver taunts the kids about the weather, laughing at the fact that they still have to go to school—no snow day. Overnight—surprise, surprise—several feet of snow is dumped on the town. Anxious children sit clustered around the radio and television praying for the cancellation of school. When the announcer prematurely announces that schools are in session, the principal responds with an "aha!" He takes pleasure in the fact that every student's dream has been dashed.

It turns out to be a snow day after all, and throughout that magical day the principal is given several opportunities to make a fool of himself in front of his students. When he first ventures from his house to shovel out his car he is attacked by snowball wielding children. He retaliates with, "You kids wanna play rough? I *invented* rough!" His exaggerated weakness belies this claim. Crouched against the barrage of snowballs he mutters to himself, "Must have the courage of ten principals; must get home." He does not succeed until much later in the movie. He spends most of the day stumbling through the snow, falling down and issuing threats like, "I'm taking names!" He finally makes it home, breathes a sigh of relief as he locks the door . . . then turns around and is pelted with another deluge of snowballs. End of movie.

In *Mighty Ducks*, the elementary principal makes only one brief, but illustrative appearance. This dour-faced old woman invites disrespect with her condescending treatment of students. When they all quack at her like a duck, she hands down the age-old punishment of writing sentences on the board, in this case, "I will not quack at the principal." When the students' hockey coach asks them in amused disbelief, "Did you really quack at the principal?" they nod their heads proudly. He responds with high fives and cheers, "Are we mighty ducks, or what?!"

I conclude my movie review with *Billy Madison*, because at this point I quit watching school-based movies. One can only take so much evidence, even when it supports your own theory. For reasons too complicated (or ridiculous) to explain, Billy Madison, an adult, has to prove himself to his rich father by repeating all twelve grades of school in twenty-four weeks. He contends that he can pass each grade in a two-week period, thus demonstrating his ability to take over his father's multimillion-dollar hotel business.

It isn't until third grade that Billy (and the viewer) are subjected to the revolting character who serves as principal of the elementary school. When the teacher is sick, Principal Anderson serves as her substitute. The pudgy man enters the classroom of unruly children and weakly commands them to, "please take your seats." He notices a student passing a note and demands (again in his high-pitched, weak voice), "Bring that note up to me. Now let's see what couldn't wait till after class." He reads the note aloud:

> We're so lucky to have Principal Anderson substituting. Now we have the privilege of staring at that tub of lard all day long. If I were him, I would walk my fat ass right into oncoming traffic.

Not only is the principal the butt (no pun intended) of student jokes, he is stupid enough to read the entire note aloud to the class. But that is not what rates him "revolting" in my book (and I mean that literally!).

On Valentine's Day the students read Valentines from their classmates. Billy Madison, adult third grader, picks up a lavishly decorated, heart-shaped card and reads the message therein:

> *I want you, Billy*
> *From: Principal Anderson*
> *p. s. I'm horny*

Billy looks up at the principal seated behind the teacher's desk. Principal Anderson gives a coy, suggestive smile, removes his glasses and nods his head. I was prepared to stop watching at that point, but I persevered.

Throughout the rest of the movie, Principal Anderson reappears in an abundance of embarrassing and compromising positions, not the least of which is his side job as a professional wrestler, aptly named the Revolting Blob. We learn that in 1983 he "sat on some guy's head and killed him." We also see Principal Anderson lolling around in a swimming pool like a beached whale, spouting water through the gap in his front teeth. On television, he lies about taking a bribe from Billy Madison. In the final scene he hugs Billy at his high school graduation and whispers in his ear, "I'm still horny."

But that's not all! This movie has *two* principals! Before Billy Madison can receive his high school diploma, he must first win an academic decathlon against the executive vice president of his father's company (I'm *not* making this up). This event begins with an inspiring speech by the high school principal:

> Thanks to a generous donation . . . I've been able to arrange for ten different teachers to administer this academic decathlon in various courses of study. However, should either contestant attempt to cheat—especially with my wife who is a dirty, dirty tramp—I am just gonna snap. Do I make myself clear?

Is it any wonder that I concluded my film research at this point?

CONCLUSION: SO, WHAT'S THE BIG DEAL?

In case you haven't counted, I have reviewed fifteen movies in this chapter. The score stands at three good principals, one borderline principal, and eleven bad principals. I believe these statistics support my initial theory that principals in film are most often portrayed in a negative light. Though I did not view every principal film ever made, I did watch nearly every film suggested to me by others, including many that didn't make this book because, although they involved schools, no principal figure was present. In my quest for titles, I asked about movies containing schools and principals; in my requests I made no distinction between good and bad principals. When all the viewing was done, the evidence strongly suggested that Hollywood's portrayal of principals leans heavily to the negative side.

The first question that comes to my mind is, why? Are the principals portrayed in film reflective of principals in the real world? Are there really more incompetent, uncaring, and cruel principals in our schools than effective, compassionate and altruistic ones? I don't believe so. Oh, I know there are some. Every profession has its share of people who are in it for the wrong reasons, who use the position for personal gain or misguided intentions, but they are surely not in the majority. Filmmakers have taken the notion of poor school leadership and exaggerated it to an astronomical degree, leading the viewer to regard principals as villainous characters. They must have their reasons.

The most obvious reason is that it pays off at the box office. Filmmakers have evidently determined that movies portraying negative principals have more appeal than those that portray positive ones. We have heard more than once that the movie industry is only giving the viewing public what it wants to see—violence, sex, non-stop action . . . and bad principals. There is likely at least some truth to this justification. I can understand that teenagers derive humor and satisfaction from seeing principals look foolish or antagonistic. The adolescent mind is often predisposed to oppose and resent adult authority figures. But what about the films aimed at an adult audience? Are adults equally attracted by situations in which authority is ridiculed and degraded? Perhaps it is a part of the *human* psyche and not just the adolescent one to distrust and criticize those in leadership positions. If so, Hollywood has simply capitalized on the opportunity to supply what the market demands.

Is that such a big deal? Why should I—or anyone else—care that principals are portrayed so negatively in film? To me it is more than just a personal affront, although that is certainly part of it. My ego takes a hit every time the profession is slighted or comes under attack. When I'm not taking it personally, I am concerned with how the negative portrayal of principals impacts schools. Might Hollywood's propensity for creating bad principals distort people's perceptions of the role? Could this distortion lead people to distrust or disrespect real principals? What affect might this have on principals' relationships with students, parents, teachers and the community?

My goal is not to answer all the questions posed above, but I offer some food for thought. The previous chapters have highlighted the significance of interpersonal relationships to school leadership. Principals who truly wish to improve students' lives (and ultimately society) through education will do so by first building and maintaining strong, positive relationships with the people they serve. They must be mindful of any obstacles to this goal. Some people carry with them preconceived notions of principals based on negative memories of real experiences. It is possible that the types of principals portrayed in film contribute to negative preconceptions as well. Principals should consider how to counteract these images and not reinforce them. Then school leaders would have a better chance of gaining the trust, admiration and respect that is critical to effective school practices.

I have a final thought on this subject. As I have described this chapter to some of my friends I have received responses like, "But, principals aren't the only ones that get short-changed in film." Well, this is certainly true. A lot of the movies I reviewed, especially those of the "teeny-bopper" genre, do little to promote the admiration of custodians, bus drivers, police officers or parents. This book is about *principals*, however, and poetic license allows me the freedom to limit my discussion. If those other groups want to write their own books, I'll be happy to supply a list of movie titles.

Chapter Seven

Principals' Reactions to What People Think Principals Do

INTRODUCTION

Throughout this book I have shared some of my own reactions to people's perceptions of the principal role. In this chapter I include the viewpoints of other practicing principals. During the research phase, I interviewed principals much as I did the other groups, asking some of the same questions. Then, when the previous chapters were written, I asked several principals to read and respond to the perceptions portrayed by students, parents, teachers, community members, and filmmakers. This chapter offers firsthand insights about what principals do and also shares principals' reactions to what other people think they do.

WHAT'S MISSING?

My principal colleagues and I were impressed at the extent to which students, parents, teachers, and others demonstrated an understanding of the principal role. They identified many of the tasks and responsibilities principals perform and recognized some of the challenges principals face. It is important to note, however, that they do so only as a collective group. No individual displayed a comprehensive understanding of all aspects of the job; it is in reviewing their *combined* responses that the principalship appears fairly well defined and interpreted. Even then, they missed or misunderstood a few important elements of the job.

Although children and adults alike recognized the many difficulties and challenges that principals face, they overlooked a crucial one—meeting the needs of a diverse and ever-changing student population. One principal defines this as "the complexity of the twenty-first century child." In addition to the once traditional two-parent home, students "come from homes with no parents, one parent, or two parents in the process of divorce." For some students, the home provides a healthy, happy environment, while for others it is a place of conflict, neglect, poverty, or violence. Those who have been principals for a long time claim that the number of students from dysfunctional or unhappy homes is growing every year.

The changing structure of the family and of society has increased the function of schools beyond simple education. For some students, schools provide the basic necessities of food (not just lunch), clothing, shelter, and healthcare. These needs must be met before students can be expected to learn. At the same time, other students come from homes where all their needs are met. They come to school ready to learn. These are the two extremes; between them lies a host of complex home situations. The challenge for schools, and thus for principals, is meeting so many diverse needs in one setting. Principals, as educational leaders, are daunted by the task of helping teachers provide a fair and equitable education to all students, given that the students' home situations are neither fair nor equitable. This is more difficult than all the paperwork, long hours, and complaints combined.

A challenge closely tied to diverse student needs is the trend toward increased accountability for student learning. Public officials, parents, and the community demand school accountability, which translates into student performance, which translates into test scores. National and state legislation continues to increase the number of high-stakes tests required of students at all levels. Schools with low student test scores are often labeled "low performing," suggesting that the teachers and the principal (as educational leader) are not doing their jobs. Many accountability measures do not *account* for other factors that affect student learning, not the least of which is the student's home life and socioeconomic background. Principals and their teaching staff know the needs of their specific student population, yet are forced to fit all students into the same box. They are pressured to emphasize test performance over other learning goals in order to prove themselves and their schools. The accountability movement has given new and not always definitive meanings to the concept of the principal as educational leader.

Very few of the people interviewed recognized another responsibility principals have inherited over the years—the need to create an environment that counteracts the effects of a society that glorifies sex, violence, and materialism. Students are bombarded by images and values that jeopardize both their physical and moral development. Society's preoccupation with sex manifests itself in students' dress and language in the early grades; by middle school and high school some students have actually begun to experiment with sexual relations. I recently read about a high school where the student elected prom queen turned out to be pregnant. The principal faced the controversial decision of whether or not to allow the girl to retain her "regal" status. This is not the type of decision a school leader should have to make.

The violence portrayed in the media finds its way into classrooms and onto the playground as students emulate what they see on a daily basis. Kindergarten students build guns from blocks and wield them at their classmates. Upper elementary students settle peer conflicts with their fists or sketch violent scenes in their notebooks. By high school, students can be either the victims or the perpetrators of gang violence. Recent school shootings have created a culture of fear and suspicion. All of these situations force principals to neglect administrative and educational duties in the interest of more immediate concerns for safety.

Finally, our materialistic society teaches that instant gratification and tangible rewards are major motivating factors. Ideally, we would like students to display appropriate and respectful behavior towards others simply because it is the right thing to do; we want them to *want* to be good people. Realistically, students often learn appropriate behavior through the imposition of negative consequences. That is no longer enough. Today's youth also expect to be rewarded for following rules and fulfilling their duties. A pat on the back or a "good job" is often not enough. They expect tokens in the form of prizes, candy and special privileges. It is not just students who have fallen prey to this way of thinking. Parents, teachers and, yes, even principals, have resorted to measures that basically bribe students to follow rules or finish their schoolwork. It is difficult to be a school leader who holds students to high standards when society encourages them to consider "what's in it for me?"

So far I have described some of the challenges facing school principals that others do not seem to adequately appreciate. What makes them challenging is they are factors outside our control and yet they greatly affect our work. There are other less critical aspects of the job that were also overlooked by the students, parents, teachers, and community members who contributed to this book.

One misunderstanding relates to the principal's role in the budgetary process. Many adults seem to think the principal is responsible for developing the school's budget. This is true for some, but for most principals budget development is handled at another level by school boards, finance councils, or district administration. School principals are basically charged with managing the budget—approving building expenditures according to pre-established parameters. Principals need to *understand* the budgetary process and may even be allowed some input, but most do not have primary control over how money is allocated. As a general rule, the bigger the school and the bigger the district, the less influence a principal has on budget design.

The same can be said of curriculum development. In most districts, the curriculum is written by a team of "experts" and passed down to the individual school level. Curricular decisions like textbook and program adoptions are also often made at the district level, though a team of school representatives may be created for this purpose. Only in autonomous institutions (like some private schools, small public systems, or alternative schools) are curricular decisions made at the individual school level and led by the principal. For many principals, the curriculum is a given; their responsibility lies in ensuring that teachers understand the curriculum and use it to guide classroom instruction.

Many adults and a few students identified the principal's need to be well versed in school law, but further conversation with some of these people suggests that they are unaware of the number and scope of laws that affect schools and students. Because schools employ people, they are required to abide by regulations associated with personnel. These include employee rights, OSHA requirements, New-Hire Reporting Laws, and state mandates regarding criminal background checks, to name a few. Principals must ensure that schools comply with these laws and regulations.

In addition, principals must have some knowledge of family law as it pertains to parental rights and custody issues. If one parent has sole custody, can the other request information about the child's progress? Are schools required to provide separate conferences for non-custodial parents? If so, does the custodial parent need to be notified? If one parent is granted a restraining order against the other, the principal needs to know how to uphold the dictates of the court ruling should the restraining order be breached. Principals face these types of situations, and if they don't know the answers they need to know where to go to find out.

There are many more laws that pertain to education, including those that deal with federal and state funding, student discipline policies, environmental issues, child abuse, sexual harassment, professional licensure, copyright, censorship, and student records. Laws related to education are so numerous, entire books are devoted to the subject. Suffice it to say that as our society increases its dependence on the role of the legal system, so do schools.

Of all the people interviewed, a very small number identified the principal's role in special education matters. Although most principals were not special education teachers themselves, they must understand and support the role of special education within the school. Special education encompasses services for students with learning disabilities, emotional or behavior disabilities, speech and language impairments, and physical impairments. These services are mandated and governed by federal legislation and are aimed at providing an equitable and non-restrictive learning environment for all students. Principals must be aware of the laws, procedures and funding associated with special education. They must ensure that teachers and special education directors follow due process when referring and assessing students for special education services. Principals also meet with the special education team and parents to develop Individual Education Plans (IEPs), which identify the needs and goals to be addressed for each special education student. Principals do not need to be experts in special education, but they need to have a broad enough knowledge of the goals and procedures to help teachers and parents understand the role of special education.

Another responsibility that very few identified is the principal's role in school-wide planning. Principals are responsible for maintaining a long-range plan that outlines goals and timelines for school improvement initiatives. The principal shares this responsibility with a site team, planning committee or some other group made up of teachers, parents and possibly community members. A unique characteristic of the principal job is that we are always operating in two worlds—the present and the future. This is especially true toward the end of the school year. I find that while I am immersed in year-end reports and events, I must simultaneously develop plans and schedules for the upcoming school year. Beginning in April I carry two calendar planners at all times, and I know my principal colleagues do the same. Both short-term and long-term planning require the principal to be always focused on where the school is headed. The challenge is to keep others focused forward as well.

Finally, one of my principal colleagues wrote, "One thing that I'd like to add to what a successful principal does all day is they spend time in reflection. The principal becomes the key player in the direction a school is heading when they take the time to listen, study, think, and formulate a plan." I believe most principals would agree. Although much of the job is hectic, and we are often called to immediate action, successful principals are also thoughtful about what they do. It is important to continually reflect on what we are doing and what we have done in order to learn from our experience and apply that learning to future situations.

NOT IN THE JOB DESCRIPTION

Principals often find themselves doing things they never envisioned would be part of the principal job. These are not tasks necessarily required of principals; they simply fall on our shoulders because they need to be done, and because there is no one else to do them at the time. Following is a list of tasks my principal colleagues and I are fairly certain most people don't realize we do:

- Help children who are hurt—give Band-Aids and give lots of hugs.
- Take sick children home; pick them up if they missed the bus.
- Clean up after sick children.
- Find clothes for children.
- Change the paper towels in the bathroom. Clean up messes when the janitor is not around.
- Wipe the windowsills in the stairwell when students begin to write their names in the dust.
- Pick up the scrap of paper that no one else notices on the floor.

- Remind the teachers that "if in doubt, throw it out" applies to the items in the staff room refrigerator.
- Check heads for lice when the nurse isn't available.
- Offer your shoulder and a box of tissues when a tearful parent comes to tell you about an impending divorce.
- Lie awake at night wondering if a child is being abused at home, or if the comment they made to you in the office was just a false accusation.
- Buy with your own money things that the school needs.
- Read a lot about teaching and parenting; suggest good books to parents and teachers.
- Get up in the middle of the night to respond to an emergency or to school alarms that are triggered—sometimes falsely.
- Visit jails when kids are arrested—even pay the bail.
- Visit hospitals and mortuaries when kids are involved.
- Attend every school event from concerts to athletic events to carnivals to bake sales, in order to show your support for the school and the students.

These tasks may not be the most important ones principals do, but they are a piece of the overall picture. Principals quickly learn that the job description they were provided at the outset is not finite; any given day might add a new item to the list of responsibilities. One principal sums it up well:

> While I clearly think that decisions surrounding the educational program are paramount to the principal's role, there are occasions when other issues take priority. For example, it might be that the lunch lines are taking longer than usual, or a student missed his bus route and parents are wondering where their child is, or a staff member is ill and needs to leave immediately. While these may appear to be mundane, a principal needs to also deal with the little things. I believe that being flexible is essential to a principal.

WHY DO IT?

With every chapter of this book the role of the principalship appears more vast, more complex, and more challenging. One principal remarked, "I don't think the general public appreciates that this job is like no other."

The other principal respondents agree that the job is a demanding one and becoming more so all the time. But that is not the complete picture. There are many rewarding and enjoyable aspects to the principalship. They are the reasons many of us were drawn to the role and remain in it. I would like to end this chapter by highlighting some of the non-tangible rewards of being a school principal.

As clichéd as it sounds, principals can make a difference. Many of us truly believe and strive for that. The principalship provides the opportunity to have a broad impact on the lives of students, their families, and entire communities. I am often asked if I like being a principal. I usually reply that I like some of the things I *do* as a principal, and even when I have a particularly difficult day I feel good knowing that I am doing important work. Obviously I don't *like* listening to complaints, and I don't *like* meeting with students about inappropriate behaviors, but I know it is important to others that problems get resolved. It is satisfying to be a part of that process. I think many of my principal colleagues agree that being a principal isn't a job you *like* so much as it is a job you feel good about.

There are so many other "little" rewards that happen on a daily basis. Writing this book has caused me to be more aware of those little things, and just today I experienced several. This morning before the opening bell rang I wandered through the halls (as we principals are wont to do) and stopped by a few classrooms. In second grade students were engaged in a variety of quiet "free time" activities, and I asked what they were doing. Three girls told me, "We're making something for you." Later that day their teacher let them bring me a handmade card that reads, "Thank you for being are [sic] principal." My first thought was, "Hey, it's payday!"

This afternoon a seventh-grade boy stopped by my office after his private drum lesson to say, "It went great." He excitedly told me that the band students were going to do a recital on Grandparents' Day (which of course he didn't realize was something *I* had set up with the band teacher!), and he showed me the music. He even plopped his drum pad on my desk and demonstrated a few moves. What made this event meaningful to me is that two weeks ago this boy had decided to quit his lessons because they took place during his math class. I spoke with the band teacher, got his lesson changed to a better time, and talked this boy into sticking with it. His visit to my office clearly tells me that I made a difference in this student's school experience, and he appreciates it.

My last example relates to a teacher issue. Today one of my teachers came to my office with a note she had received from a concerned parent. She wasn't sure how to respond to it, so we talked about it and I suggested how I would respond. Later she stopped by to let me know she had called the parent and everything was fine. Once again I felt I had provided the help that someone needed. The teacher felt better because she had handled the situation appropriately, and the parent was happy that the concern had been promptly addressed.

These are some examples from my own practice; there are so many others that happen to other principals every day. Principals who care about the people they serve *will* make a difference—a *positive* difference—and sometimes people will come right out and show you how. These are the types of experiences most principals live for. They are more gratifying than the paycheck, the "prestige," and the free coffee!

Somehow this fulfilling aspect of the principalship needs to be better communicated to other people, especially teachers. Our country is currently experiencing a principal shortage. This situation is unlikely to improve if more teachers don't aspire to become principals, and they aren't going to aspire to this position if they don't perceive it as a rewarding and worthwhile one. The teachers who contributed to this book indicated that the rewards of money, prestige and leaving the classroom are not adequate incentives for becoming a principal, nor should they be. People should choose to become principals for a host of altruistic reasons, and because they recognize the intangible rewards that this job provides.

Since only principals understand what those intangible rewards are, perhaps we are called upon to communicate them to others. We need to talk positively about our work and the feelings of fulfillment and self-worth it awards us. We must encourage talented and dedicated teachers to consider expanding their service to a leadership position where they can have a broad impact on students, on schools and on entire communities. If we are to have enough qualified, dedicated people to lead our schools we must not allow the positive aspects of the principalship to be the best kept secret in our profession.

Chapter Eight

Final Thoughts

WHAT HAVE WE LEARNED?

This book has uncovered perceptions people have of what principals do. At the same time, it has also helped *me* to better understand what principals do—and has suggested what principals could do better. It should do the same for all who read it. A key point I would like to make about the principal role is that there is no single description of what principals do, no definitive list of principal responsibilities that applies to all principals. Principals all share some common responsibilities, but some aspects of the role differ across settings.

A major factor affecting the principal role is the size of the school. Principals in large schools have more people to serve, so they have more people with whom to share the administrative and leadership duties. They may have an assistant principal, a dean of students, a curriculum director—or several of each. In a large school the principal may not handle daily discipline issues or be responsible for classroom observations of teachers. That doesn't mean their job is easier; in many ways it is more difficult. A large school means more people to know, more paperwork to do, more problems to solve, more phone calls to make, more programs to oversee—more everything. Even though they have an administrative team with whom they share the load, the principal is still the ultimate leader, the one responsible for seeing that others carry out their duties.

Principals in small schools, on the other hand, tend to go it alone. At most, they may have an assistant principal, but some are the sole administrator in their building. Though the magnitude of the job is less, the breadth of responsibilities is greater. In addition to the all the administrative duties, small school principals are also more likely to spend time in the lunchroom, on the playground, or at the curb when buses arrive. This is partly because they have more time and partly because there is no one else to whom they can delegate.

From the principal's point of view, there are pros and cons for both large and small schools. From the viewpoint of students, parents, and teachers, however, small schools are more conducive to effective school leadership. The children and adults interviewed for this book place a lot of value on the interpersonal aspects of school principalship. They think principals should spend more time interacting with people throughout the school. Their favorite principals are those who are visible, available, and actively involved with students, parents and teachers. Meeting these expectations is much more difficult in a large school. There are more people with whom to interact and less time to do it. In a school of 200 students, the principal can know the name of every student, teacher and parent. In a school of 2000, this is next to impossible. Large schools simply do not allow principals to have the amount of human contact that small schools do.

The perceptions conveyed by this book also indicate that the principal role is different in elementary schools than it is in middle schools or high schools. Elementary principals tend to have more positive student interaction. They are more likely to be known by students and parents. They are more visible. This may be true for several reasons. Perhaps secondary principals place less emphasis on visibility and interaction. Perhaps the structure of secondary schools does not allow for the types of interactions that elementary schools do (playground and bus duty are no longer part of the picture). I believe the primary reason, however, points right back to school size. Middle schools and high schools tend to be larger than elementary schools. Secondary principals are usually responsible for greater numbers of students and teachers than their elementary school counterparts. Consequently they are less likely to develop relationships with *all* the people they serve. It is likely that school size has more impact on the principal role than school level does.

This is an important point for school systems to consider. School size is a hot topic in American education today. Proponents of larger schools cite better facilities and expanded student opportunities as advantages. Those in favor of small schools emphasize the importance of a close-knit, family environment where students feel like people rather than numbers. Recent school tragedies like the one at Columbine High School have fueled the fire in favor of smaller schools. In large schools, students can feel disconnected from the people around them. Teachers and principals do not get to know students on a personal level, and thus are less likely to notice the warning signs of depression, anger, or apathy. We are only beginning to recognize the impact that human interaction has on student achievement and school success. The viewpoints shared in this book take us a step closer.

Regardless of school size, setting, or any other demographic, however, I think the most important thing this book can teach us about the principalship is that it is an important job, not one to be taken lightly. The job is not for everyone. Those who choose to be principals should be interested in the betterment of others more than themselves. They should have the desire to be a positive force in the field of education and in the lives of students, families, and staff. To strive for less than that is to cheat a great many people, and to cheat yourself of the opportunity to truly make a difference.

WHERE DO WE GO FROM HERE?

Writing this book has caused me to think more critically about my role as a principal. I no longer wonder what people think I do. Instead I wonder what I can do better. I credit one of my principal colleagues for helping me make this transition. After reading the first five chapters of this book he wrote:

> I've always believed there's a general lack of understanding of the scope of the job, . . . but our job isn't to make sure everyone understands our scope; it's to do the very best we can to enhance the opportunities for student success.

I challenge all who read this book to keep this focus.

If you are a principal or hope to be one some day, I end this book with some questions and comments to spur your thinking. If you are a student, a parent, a teacher, or a member of the greater community, I hope you have found in this book some answers to your own questions about principals and the work they do—and, yes, there *is* a principal school!

Questions and Comments for Principals

- Of all the things you do in the course of a day, a week, a year, which do you believe are the most important? Is this reflected in your practice? Is this important to others as well?
- What would you most like other people to understand about your role? Why? What can you do to better communicate this to others?
- Why did you choose to become a principal? How do your reasons affect the type of leadership you provide in your school?
- Do you still want to be a principal?
- How much of your time is spent isolated in your office, and how much is spent interacting with others? How might you strengthen your relationships with students, teachers, parents and the community?
- If your office is a mysterious or intimidating place, consider how you can change that.
- Call parents for positive reasons.
- Teach a class now and then. Remember what it's like to be a teacher, to be a student.
- Be reflective about your work—take time to think about what you are doing, why you are doing it, and how you could do it better.
- The best answer to the question, "Are you busy?" is, "Yes, but I'm not too busy to talk to you."

Questions and Comments for Aspiring Principals

All of the above, plus:

- What do you expect to be most challenging in your future role as a school principal? How will you deal with this challenge?
- Who was your favorite principal? Will you display those same characteristics?
- Why do you want to be a principal? What are you hoping to gain or achieve?
- If you think the principalship is a good way to get out of the classroom, please find another way.
- If you want to be a principal because you care about students and want to work for school improvement, good for you! We need more leaders like you.
- P.S. The coffee isn't free; the hugs are.

About the Author

Sharon H. Pristash is the principal of St. James Catholic School, a K–8 school in Duluth, Minnesota. In addition to her principal duties, she has served as the part-time kindergarten teacher at St. James for the past four years. In September 2001, she received the Educator of the Year award from the Diocese of Duluth.

She was born in Portage, Wisconsin, where she lived for most of her childhood. She received her undergraduate degree in elementary education and English from The College of St. Scholastica in Duluth, Minnesota. After ten years of elementary school teaching she returned to St. Scholastica to pursue a master's degree in curriculum and instruction. She earned her K–12 administrative licensure and a doctorate degree in educational leadership from the University of St. Thomas in St. Paul, Minnesota.

Prior to her principalship at St. James, she served for three years as an instructor and field-experience supervisor in the education department at St. Scholastica, where she continues to do adjunct work. She is an active member of Phi Delta Kappa, the Association for Supervision and Curriculum Development, and the National Association of Elementary School Principals. She also sits on several professional committees in her community. She lives in Duluth with her husband of seventeen years, Robert Pristash.